The Delegates of 1849

Contents

Preface		ix
Introduction		xi
PART I. LOS ANGELES DISTRICT		
1.	Manuel Dominguez	3
2.	José Antonio Carrillo	9
3.	Abel Stearns	15
4.	Hugo Reid	25
5.	Stephen Clark Foster	37
PART II. MONTEREY DISTRICT		
6.	Thomas Oliver Larkin	45
7.	Pacificus Ord	53
8.	Lewis Dent	57
9.	Charles Tyler Botts	63
10.	Henry Wager Halleck	69

PART III. SACRAMENTO DISTRICT

11. John Augustus Sutter 77
12. Lansford Warren Hastings 85
13. Elisha Oscar Crosby 89
14. Jacob Renk Snyder 99
15. Morton Matthew McCarver 105
16. John McDougal 109
17. Winfield Scott Sherwood 111
18. William Edward Shannon 117

PART IV. SAN DIEGO DISTRICT

19. Miguel de Pedrorena 127
20. Henry James Hill 129

PART V. SAN FRANCISCO DISTRICT

21. Edward Gilbert 135
22. Elias Joseph Hobson 141
23. Francis James Lippitt 145
24. Myron Norton 155
25. Rodman McCamley Price 161
26. William McKendree Gwin 167
27. William Morris Steuart 175
28. Alfred James Ellis 179

PART VI. SAN JOAQUIN DISTRICT

29.	John McHenry Hollingsworth	*189*
30.	James McHall Jones	*205*
31.	Benjamin Franklin Moore	*211*
32.	Benjamin S. Lippincott	*215*
33.	Thomas Lloyd Vermeule	*219*
34.	Oliver Meredith Wozencraft	*223*

PART VII. SAN JOSE DISTRICT

35.	Antonio Maria Pico	*231*
36.	Joseph Aram	*235*
37.	(Willard) Julian Hanks	*239*
38.	Kimball Hale Dimmick	*243*
39.	Elam Brown	*249*
40.	Pierre Sainsevain	*255*
41.	Jacob Durant Hoppe	*259*

PART VIII. SAN LUIS OBISPO DISTRICT

42.	Henry Amos Tefft	*267*
43.	José Maria Covarrubias	*273*

PART IX. SANTA BARBARA DISTRICT

44.	Pablo de la Guerra	*279*
45.	Jacinto Rodriguez	*285*

PART X. SONOMA DISTRICT

46. Robert Baylor Semple *289*
47. Joel Pickens Walker *301*
48. Mariano Guadalupe Vallejo *305*
    Reference Sources *313*

Preface

Sometimes, a book chooses you.

On a bright afternoon in October 2013, I visited Monterey's historic Colton Hall to peruse their archives for interesting tidbits I might use in writing my historical fiction short stories. Although I had an appointment to do research for an unrelated project, the docent, Jeff Landsman, kindly took me on a tour of the very room where the 1849 Constitutional Convention was held. I admit his talk was interesting, but my focus was not on men and politics.

When he finished, I did what most writers do and asked how many books had been written exclusively about California's first Constitutional Convention. None, Jeff said. It has been overshadowed in literature by the wild and crazy Gold Rush, and the devastating Civil War.

Driving home, still determined to write my short stories about women during the late 1800s, I briefly considered writing a book about California's strategy to overcome the chaos. Before committing to the project, I wanted to review available reference sources. Thanks to the Internet, that was easy.

Every Google query brought up an abundance of primary source information from renown authors and institutions. Especially interesting was the *Report of the debates in the Convention of*

California, on the formation of the state constitution, in September and October 1849 by John Ross Browne, official reporter, published in 1850. (Browne received $10,000 to record each day's proceedings, transcribe his shorthand into sufficient copies to be approved at the next morning's session, and have the entire proceedings published in book form.) Archive.org offered a scanned version of that book in full text, Kindle and PDF, available to download for free. The text read like a screenplay.

I recalled standing in the very room where those debates took place over 164 years ago. I remembered Jeff's stories, my fingertips touching the edge of the inkwell that held writing quills. I got the chills.

The decision was made, I would write a book, perhaps a historical fiction novel with the Convention as a backdrop.

After three years of methodical research, I realized there were no characters or fiction plots that could compete with the real-life stories of those 48 men who came to Monterey and spent six weeks debating and drafting the first Constitution.

This book is dedicated to my son, Geoffrey Davis, and grandsons, Dalton and Brennan. Thank-you, boys.

Laura Emerson
San Luis Obispo, California
June 2019

Introduction

California has 39.6 million residents, making it the most populous state in the U.S. If it were a sovereign nation, the $2.8 trillion economy (2017) would be the fifth largest in the world. Agricultural output exceeds all other states. According to Bloomberg's 2019 United States Innovation Index, California ranks as the most innovative economy in the U.S.—in research and development intensity, productivity, technology companies, STEM jobs, populous with degrees in science and engineering disciplines and patent activity. When did this reputation for bold and independent action begin?

California's reputation as a bold and independent state began in 1849—as self-preservation. Congress had failed through three sessions to decide how to admit California into the Union while anarchy prevailed from the Sierra Nevada to Los Angeles with the onslaught of thousands of desperate gold-seekers.

The following newspaper editorials provide the backstory.

January 4, 1849. Provisional Government. The recent, large and unanimous meetings in the Pueblo de San Jose and in this town [San Francisco], in favor of immediate action for the establishment of a Provisional Government, are believed to be a fair index of the feeling of the community throughout the Territory — That some steps should be taken to provide a Government for the country, in the event that the U. S. Congress fail to do so at the present session [while it debates whether California should be admitted as a free state or a slave state], is obvious;

It certainly is not necessary, in calling public attention to this matter, that we should point out the insecurity of our present position. Recent events have made that fact too sadly familiar. What, then, can we urge to induce action and exertion? If the dangers we all run be not enough to induce the staid, reputable and responsible people of the country to come forward and unite as one man to build up a form of Provisional Government which will preserve the rights of, and meet out justice to, all, we shall then be obliged to continue our present system of "Lynch Law" — a system that, in its best features, is only worthy of barbarians — a system that is without a controlling power — without a steadfast guide, and that is therefore liable to fluctuate as the public feeling that directs it changes — a system that, having no settled rule of action, is as likely to turn its destroying hands against the good as the bad.

Some have asked "Why put off the day of the assembling of the Convention until the first Monday in March?" We answer, first, because that length of time will be necessary for enabling the largest part of the Territory to be represented; Second: by that time it is extremely probable we shall be in possession of information from Washington which will at once satisfy us whether there be or be not necessity for action on our part; and Third: the public mind is in want of time to digest and settle the various points that are likely to arise in so important a proceeding, in order that the delegates may come to the Convention prepared to carry out the wishes of their constituents.

The people of the different districts in making up their delegations should not forget that a Provisional Government, if forged, will be a government for all, and that consequently the Convention should be composed of men from all classes and nations. This fact is more particularly applicable to the Californians [native born of Spanish blood], and we would recommend as a highly proper course that measures be taken to engage them in the work, and that they be invited to unite in the cause by placing on the tickets the names of some one or more of the most intelligent and reputable Californians in the various parts of the country. Let all be made to understand that a Provisional Government is not a government for Americans alone, but that every bona fide resident in California is equally interested in, and should exert his influences for, the promotion of so good a cause. The delegates from the [ten] different districts should come prepared to give a full and fair expression to the wishes of those they represent,

Had there been no discovery of gold at Sutter's Mill, there would be no desperate urgency for a government and laws.

January 25, 1849. Provisional Government. Meeting at Sacramento City. At a meeting held in Sacramento City, on the 6th day of January 1849, to take into consideration the necessity and propriety of organizing a Provisional Government for the Territory of California,

Whereas, the Territory of California, having by a treaty of peace, [referring to the Treaty of Guadalupe Hidalgo, February 2, 1848] been ceded to the United States; and the recommendation of the President to Congress to extend the laws of the United States over this Territory has not been acted upon by that body[nearly one year later]; and the citizens of this territory are thus left without any laws for the protection of their lives and property; And whereas, the frequency and impunity with which robberies and murders have of late been committed, have deeply impressed us with the necessity of having some regular form of government, with laws and officers to enforce the observance of those laws;

And whereas, the discovery of large quantities of gold has attracted, and in all probability will continue to attract, an immense immigration from all parts of the world, as well as from the United

States, thus adding to the present state of confusion, and presenting temptations to crime;

By recent intelligence from Washington and other parts of the United States, it appears that the probabilities are in favor of the passage at the present session of Congress of a bill establishing a Territorial Government over us. ... As this session of Congress is a limited one by the Constitution, expiring on the fourth day of March 1849, it strikes us that the first day of May will be a sufficient postponement to allow information from Washington to reach us before the assembling of the Convention. The ocean steamers between this [San Francisco] Port and Panama, which are confidently expected to be in regular operation by that time, will bring us intelligence from Washington in thirty days. A postponement, therefore, until the first of May, will put it beyond the contingency of further change.

Congress, in the meantime, hastily presented a bill recognized as *ultra vires*, (beyond its authority), which nullified their effort. For the *third time*, a session of Congress adjourned without having decided California's status.

March 29, 1849. Proceedings of Congress. — It was proposed on the opening of Congress, to admit [Alta] California and New Mexico into the Union immediately as one State. [The original Alta California included all of what is now California, Nevada and Utah, and parts of Arizona, Wyoming, and Colorado.] But it was soon discovered that Congress's power extended to only receive States applying for admission into the Union — they had no authority to create a State. Senator Douglass, of Illinois, has therefore withdrawn his bill admitting California and New Mexico as a State, and has presented one to establish governments therein, and to provide for their organization into States whenever they shall have the requisite population. No action has yet been taken on the bill in either House. Interminable debates on the slavery question or other abstractions, continue the order of the day in Congress.

May 03, 1849. A Provisional Government. — It now becomes a matter of necessity with the people of California, to decide whether they will longer allow this country to remain without a Government. The present state of anarchy (for we can call it nothing less) is much to be deplored and is easily remedied, by united, vigorous and immediate action. We therefore recommend that public meetings be at once held in the various districts for the appointment of delegates to a Convention to form a state provisional government, and that such Convention be held at the earliest practicable day. What say you, citizens of San Francisco?

The Consistency of the "Model Republic." — Among all the misdeeds committed by the United States Congress since the foundation of the Republic, there is not one that throws a darker shade upon our national history than the outrage they have committed on the rights of the people of California in passing a revenue act to tax them, without making the slightest return for such taxation in the establishment of a government. It is a burning disgrace that men should prate so loudly of patriotism, of liberty, and of the principles and glory of the revolution which separated us from the mother country, and yet by an act like this falsify the whole theory of a Republican Government. And it will be still worse, if the people of California do not rise as one man and express their indignation in tones not to be mistaken or unheeded by the next Congress nor by the people of the United States.

Enter Brevet Brigadier General Bennet C. Riley, who assumed command as California's provincial governor on April 13, 1849. Less than two months later, with the assistance of his secretary of state and brilliant military strategist, Henry Halleck, he issued the following Proclamation calling for a Constitutional Convention.

PROCLAMATION

To the People of California. ... As Congress has failed to organise a new Territorial Government it becomes our imperative duty to take some active measures to provide for the existing wants of the country. ... [A] convention, in which all parts of the Territory are represented, shall meet and frame a State Constitution or a Territorial organization to be submitted to the people for their ratification and then proposed to Congress for its approval. Considerable time will necessarily elapse before any new government can be legitimately organised and put in operation; ...

In order to complete this organization with the least possible delay, the undersigned, in virtue of power in him vested, does hereby appoint the first of August next as the day for holding a special election for Delegates to a general Convention, ...

The general Convention for forming a State Constitution or a plan for Territorial government, will consist of thirty-seven Delegates who will meet in Monterey on the first day of September next. ... The local Alcaldes and members of the Ayuntamientos or Town Councils will act as Judges and Inspectors of elections. ... The polls will be open from 10 o'clock A.M. to 4 P.M., or until sun set if the Judges deem it necessary.

Every free male citizen of the United States and Upper California, twenty-one years of age, and actually resident in the district where the vote is offered, will be entitled to the right of suffrage. All citizens of Lower California who have been forced to come to this territory on account of having rendered assistance to the American troops during the recent war with Mexico, should also be allowed to vote in the district where they actually reside. Great care should be taken by the Inspectors that votes are received only from bona fide citizens actually resident in the country. These judges and Inspectors previous to entering upon the duties of their office, should take an oath faithfully and truly to perform these duties. The returns should state distinctly the number of votes received for each candidate, be signed

The Delegates of 1849

by the Inspectors, sealed and immediately transmitted to the Secretary of State for file in his office. ...

The method here indicated to attain what is desired by all, viz: a more perfect political organization, is deemed the most direct and safe that can be adopted, and one fully authorised by law. ... It is therefore hoped that it will meet the approbation of the people of California, and that all good citizens will unite in carrying it into execution.

Given at Monterey, California, this third day of June, A. D. 1849. (Signed) B. RILEY, Brevet Brig Genl. USA, and Governor of California. Official—H. W. HALLECK, Bvt. Capt. and Secretary of State.

Governor Riley did not have the authority to call a constitutional convention—but he did it anyway. The delegates did not have the authority to declare California a state or draw its boundary—but they did it anyway.

The Territory was divided into ten districts with the number of delegates determined by population. Seventy-two men were elected, only 48 came to Monterey. They were lawyers, merchants, ranchers, military officers, printers, surveyors, bankers, and physicians. Not everyone spoke English. Many were strangers to each other while some had been business partners or friends—or adversaries—for years.

They worked diligently six days a week for six weeks to draft California's first Constitution. Following the Convention, elections were held for governor, lieutenant governor, senators, and assemblymen to the first state legislature, proposed to meet two months later on December 15, 1849.

Only one other time in U.S. history has a body of dedicated representatives acted with such mature determination and self-reliance to form its own government. Philadelphia, 1787.

LAURA EMERSON

Each delegate's life is a story worth telling.

PART I

Los Angeles District

1

Manuel Dominguez

On November 19, 1877, Don Manuel welcomed Thomas Savage into his home with the same gracious dignity he offered to all his visitors. He read the letters of introduction Thomas presented, encouraging him to allow Thomas to interview him for Hubert Howe Bancroft's "History of California." As former U.S. consul to Cuba, Thomas understood the fine art of diplomacy and was fluent in Spanish. What Thomas didn't realize was that he was dealing with a man whose own grasp of diplomacy was far more skillful than his own. Don Manuel and his vast land holdings had survived and thrived through the Spanish, Mexican and American conquests.

The 74-year-old humbly insisted that his many years away from public life and a failing memory might cause him to provide incorrect and misleading information. He would not have his name associated with false assertions. Thomas then asked Don Manuel about the historical documents in his possession, asking outright for him to donate them to the Bancroft collection. Don

Manuel's polite response was that he had no records of a public nature.

Was Don Manuel genuinely fearful of giving false information, or was there another reason? Did he perhaps believe that talking about those early days would be disloyal to the memories of his family and friends? Loyalty and devotion were at the heart of Don Manuel's life—loyalty to his family, his country, his religion, and his beloved Rancho San Pedro.

Born on January 26, 1803, at Mission San Juan Capistrano, Don Manuel was the third Dominquez to own Rancho San Pedro. His father, Cristóbal, inherited the land from his uncle, Juan José, a Spanish soldier with the Gaspar de Portola Expedition that escorted Friar Junipero Serra to Alta California. He retired from the military in 1784 and petitioned the provincial governor for vacant land south of the Pueblo de Los Angeles where he could raise cattle. The governor was Juan José's former lieutenant. For his years of loyal military service, he received the first private land grant in Southern California. Rancho San Pedro was 75,000 acres or 120 square miles. (It included what is today the entire Port of Los Angeles, San Pedro, Harbor City, Wilmington, Carson, Compton, Dominguez Hills, Lomita, Palos Verdes Peninsula, Redondo Beach, Hermosa Beach, Manhattan Beach, and Torrance.)

Twenty-one years later, blind and with no family of his own, Juan José went to live with his nephew, Cristóbal. When Juan José died in 1809, Cristóbal inherited half of Rancho San Pedro. He was a career military officer who had no interest in ranching. Shortly before his death in 1822, Cristóbal made out a simple will, bequeathing the land to his children.

As the eldest surviving male child, 19-year-old Manuel was

now head of the family. With no interest in pursuing a military career, he moved his mother and siblings, along with a small herd of cattle, to their new home at Rancho San Pedro. As a cattle rancher, Manuel came into frequent contact with American traders. He became fluent in English—speaking, reading and writing—skills which enabled him to excel as a rancher and a businessman.

When Alta California came under Mexican control, everyone who had received land grants under the previous Spanish rule was ordered to present proof of land ownership to the Mexican government if they were to keep their land. Don Manuel was one of the few who had such evidence. In 1826, the Dominguez family received confirmation that the Mexican government re-granted the Rancho to Cristóbal Dominguez and his heirs.

A year later, 24-year-old Manuel and 21-year-old Maria De Gracia Cota were joined in holy matrimony at the San Gabriel Mission. They would be married for 55 years, living all that time at Rancho San Pedro where they would raise their 10 children and remain devout followers of the teachings of the Roman Catholic Church.

Don Manuel's plan to spend his life on his rancho was disrupted the following year when the community leaders asked him to join them in local government, a role that would last for 16 years. He first accepted a seat on the Town Council of Los Angeles. That same year he was appointed presidential elector representing the Pueblo de Los Angeles and the following year he was a delegate to the first Mexican legislature in Alta California.

He was elected to three separate terms as alcalde of Los Angeles in 1832, 1839 and 1842. From 1833 to 1836 he was auxiliary alcalde of the Pueblo. In 1834 he served as a member of the assembly of Alta California. In 1836, and again in 1843, he was elected justice of the peace, representing an area that included his own Rancho San Pedro. In 1843, he was also appointed prefect of the Second District of Los Angeles, the highest political office in the area because he reported directly to the governor. The position was abolished the following year, which enabled Don Manuel to finally retire to private life, away from the revolutionary politics of the day. But, the revolution came to him.

In 1846, American military forces invaded Alta California and captured the Pueblo de Los Angeles. A garrison of 50 American troops was stationed there to maintain order. The local citizens reacted to the harsh restrictions placed on them by quickly organizing a rebellion. On September 30, the Americans were forced out of town and retreated to San Pedro, but not before sending word to the commander of U.S. military forces in California about the so-called resistance. Several hundred soldiers were dispatched to retake El Pueblo de Los Angeles.

The reinforcement soldiers met resistance from about 20 Californio horsemen armed with lances, who subjected them to their rapid "hit and run" tactics. Nearing Rancho San Pedro, the American officers decided to stay there for the night. Viewing all Californios as the enemy, the troops marched onto Don Manuel's property and seized all the ranch buildings except the Dominguez adobe. The family was ordered to provide food and supplies to the American invaders. Don Manuel sent a messenger to Los Angeles notifying the Mexican officials about the American reinforcements.

Just before midnight, nearly 100 Californios, led by future convention delegate, José Antonio Carrillo, arrived to challenge the invaders. Guns were fired into the air all night long to disturb the

Americans. At sunrise, José Antonio fired a cannon that damaged the roof of the Dominguez adobe. The trespassers quickly packed up and left.

Don Manuel was a formidable presence at the Constitutional Convention. He was a wealthy and well-respected California native, familiar with the American way of doing business. While he made no public comment or participated in any of the debates, the records indicate he was in attendance and voted throughout the entire six weeks.

After the Convention, Don Manuel returned once again to private life. When the devastating drought years of the 1860s saw other rancheros lose everything, Rancho San Pedro survived. Long before the drought years, Don Manuel had diversified his operations and grew alfalfa, barley, beans, and oats to supplement his cattle business.

Don Manuel died on October 11, 1882, at the age of 79. Doña Maria, his beloved wife, died the following year. Rancho San Pedro was partitioned among their six surviving children, all daughters. Maria Susana lived in Los Angeles where she and her husband were members of Saint Vibiana's Catholic Church. Her parents had been generous patrons of Saint Vibiana's for many years.

After moving to Redondo Beach, once part of Rancho San Pedro, Susana persuaded a priest from St. Vibiana's to come to their home and offer Mass every Sunday, inviting neighbors to join them. When the congregation outgrew their home, the Dominguez sisters donated land and money for the construction of Saint James Catholic Church, to be built in Redondo Beach in memory of their parents. The first Mass was held in 1892. As of September 2017, Saint James Catholic Church in Redondo Beach has 5,948 registered families, or 15,058 members, and celebrated its 125th anniversary.

Throughout his life, Don Manuel resisted selling any land, preferring instead to lease parcels and retain ownership. This strategy has been followed by his descendants. Today, they are owners of the Watson Land Company, founded in 1912 and Carson Companies, which states on its website that it "traces its roots back to the Dominguez family land grant awarded more than 230 years ago" on the original Rancho land.

In the early 1960s, stockholders of the Dominguez Estate Company voted to sell off a portion of their land, offering 1,808 acres for $58.5 million. The sale was the largest in Southern California history. The State of California purchased a section of the property, and the Board of Trustees of the California State Universities voted to build a new campus on the west side of Dominguez Hills. Today California State University at Dominguez Hills is one of the most ethnically and economically diverse universities in the western United States.

The original Dominguez home, located in Compton, is a California historical landmark. The adobe contains much of the original furniture. Perhaps there's a locked desk somewhere that holds those papers Don Manuel refused to show Thomas Savage.

2

José Antonio Carrillo

José Antonio also came from a prominent military family. His great-grandfather was born at the Loretto Presidio in 1680. His father, José Raymundo, marched with the Portola Expedition and enjoyed a distinguished military career, serving as commandant of the San Diego Presidio. Two of José Antonio's older brothers likewise distinguished themselves with military careers. This future delegate followed a different path.

José Antonio was born in 1796 at Mission Dolores in San Francisco, the seventh of eight children. As an adult, José Antonio was said to be endowed with exceptional natural abilities. He also had a reputation as a gambler, a man of loose habits, and reckless in his associations. There was always a plot on hand or a revolution underway.

Is it possible that he was considered for a military career but found to be lacking essential prerequisites? Did his father's death when José Antonio was 12 years old influence his maturity? Was his volatile behavior an attempt to prove that he was as good a soldier as his father and brothers?

Some historical resources say his first employment was as a schoolteacher, and that an argument ended that career. What is certain is that José Antonio was a complicated man.

In 1823, he married his first wife, Maria Estefana Pico, sister of Pio Pico (the last governor of Alta California) when he was 27, and she was 17. His brother, Domingo Antonio Carrillo, commandant of the Santa Barbara Presidio in the early 1830s, was also married to a sister of Pio Pico.

Records indicate José Antonio was alcalde of Los Angeles in 1826, 1828, and 1833.

In 1834, Mexican Governor José Figueroa granted him the 26,623-acre Rancho Las Posas in what is now Ventura County. In 1842, he sold the land to his sister's husband, José de la Guerra. The following year, Mexican Governor Manuel Micheltorena, granted José Antonio and his brother, Carlos Antonio, the 53,195-acre Island of Santa Rosa, the second-largest of the Channel Islands. Carlos's daughters and their husbands were given authority to manage the island.

In 1836, José Antonio went to Mexico as a delegate to the Mexican Congress. He was on a personal mission. The Mexican government was planning to send 1,200 soldiers into Alta California in retaliation for yet another rebellious attempt at independence.

José Antonio persuaded the supreme government that it was unnecessary and expensive to send soldiers to Alta California. He had a better idea. The Alta Californians wanted native sons to govern them because these men knew their countrymen and were aware of the needs of California. He proposed that his brother, Carlos Antonio Carillo, be appointed the governor, replacing the current Governor Alvarado. The Mexican Congress liked his idea and drew up the appointment of Carlos Antonio as interim governor, authorizing him to set up his own government.

In 1840, José Antonio's wife, Estefana, died. Two years later he married another sister of Pio Pico, Maria Jacinta. He was 45 years old, and she was 27. She died the following year. In May 1846, 50-year-old José Antonio married for a third time to 20-year-old Francisca Leona Sepulveda. This marriage would also end, but for a different reason.

It was José Antonio to whom Don Manuel sent the message about the American troops invading his rancho. He knew José Antonio could rouse a militia at a moment's notice, but he never expected him to fire a cannon at his home. Still, it had its effect. The American troops quickly mobilized and continued their northward advance.

Other battles in other locations took place between the Mexican and American forces. On January 10, 1847, the Pueblo of Los Angeles was captured by the Americans for the last time. On January 13th, José Antonio, acting as a commissioner for Mexico, is credited with drafting the Treaty of Cahuenga, in English and Spanish, and being present at the signing.

While José Antonio's remarks during the Constitutional Convention might be considered controversial, he believed he was representing the wishes of his constituents. He spoke through an interpreter.

Sept. 5: Mr. Carrillo stated that he represented one of the most respectable communities in California, and he did not believe it to be to the interest of his constituents that a State Government should be formed. At the same time, as a great majority of this Convention appeared to be in favor of a State Government, he proposed that the country should be divided by running a line west from San Luis Obispo, so that all north of that line might have a State Government, and all south thereof a Territorial Government. He and his colleagues were under instructions to vote for a Territorial Government although a gentleman belonging to this body had stated, that it was not the object of the Convention to form a constitution for the Californians, he begged leave to say, that he considered himself as much an American citizen as the gentleman who made the assertion.

Sept 15: Mr. Carrillo rose, to address the Convention, and the Interpreter and Interpreter's Clerk being absent, Mr. Foster, a member from Los Angeles, was requested to interpret the remarks of Mr. Carrillo complained of incompetency and disrespectful language on the part of the Interpreter's Clerk, whereupon Mr. Botts moved the following, Resolved, that on the complaint of Mr. Carrillo, a member of this House, of indignity offered to him, in his seat, by the interpreter's clerk, the said clerk be removed. The resolution was adopted.

In 1853, José Antonio's third marriage ended. Instead of dying, Francisca divorced him.

> The testimony was closed on Saturday at dark, and the argument of the case occupied the whole of Monday. The jury, after about an hour's retirement, returned a special verdict, finding that the defendant is habitually intemperate, and has willfully neglected for three years to provide the common necessities for his wife, having the ability to do so. They also found that the plaintiff had always conducted herself as a faithful and affectionate wife; and the value of defendant's property—a house and lot in the city of Los Angeles—to be

worth $5,000. The court instructed the jury as follows, viz: ... The decree of the court was rendered on Thursday, declaring plaintiff and defendant divorced from the bonds of matrimony, and awarding to plaintiff alimony in the sum of $400 per annum, during her natural life, payable quarterly; the same being a charge and lien upon said house and lot, with execution therefore, or for any installments, if unpaid; besides $150 for attorney's fee and cost of suit.

José Antonio had been a leader in the revolution that deposed Governor Victoria. He plotted against Governor Alvarado and was instrumental in the overthrow of Governor Micheltorena. His charismatic personality enabled him to associate with prominent individuals. Yet, he involved himself with unsavory characters in Santa Barbara where he died in 1862 at the age of 66.

There was nothing José Antonio would not do to oblige a friend or get the better of a foe, using every means possible to carry out his plans.

3

Abel Stearns

Abel had been living in California for 20 years before the Constitutional Convention convened. In that time, he accumulated the largest cash fortune and the most land. But few people called him their friend.

Abel was born on February 9, 1798, in Lunenburg Massachusetts where his ancestors had been farmers for five generations. In late 1810, Abel and his six siblings were orphaned when their parents tragically died within three months of each other. There was no money to provide for the children; likely, no relative or family friend who could take them all.

Whose decision was it that within a year of his parents' deaths 13-year-old Abel was taken to Boston and put aboard a merchant sailing ship? For the next 15 years, he would sail on several trading vessels, visiting ports in China, the East Indies, the West Indies, and Spanish America. He not only matured on the high seas but was educated there as well.

In 1826, Abel settled in Mexico and became a naturalized Mexican citizen. In 1829, he sailed to Monterey California where he met fellow merchant Thomas Larkin who was a representative for Captain Cooper's Monterey Trading Company. Abel and Larkin would become lifelong friends.

In 1831, Abel was sent to El Pueblo de Los Angeles as a representative for Captain Cooper's Monterey Trading Company. Two years later, he was the Los Angeles partner of Don Juan Bandini, a wealthy San Diego merchant. This was only the beginning of their relationship.

As El Pueblo de Los Angeles was becoming California's most populous town, Abel quickly became its most prosperous trader. Cargo ships sailed up and down the coast, stopping in ports long enough to sell their merchandise from onboard stores. Having shoppers come aboard the ships was entertaining for everyone but economically inefficient. There was a real need for fixed, independent merchants—and Abel seized the opportunity.

He opened a trading and mercantile store in San Pedro, selling exotic and conventional merchandise to local citizens, and collecting cattle hides as payment. He then sold the hides to sea merchants at a considerable profit. The following year, he used those profits to purchase land. His first real estate investment was a lot near downtown Los Angeles. His dream was to build the most magnificent adobe on the Plaza. He also bought property in San Pedro that included an old adobe warehouse with a fascinating history.

After receiving permission in 1821 from Mexican Governor Alvarado, trading partners William Hartnell and Hugh McCulloch erected the first warehouse in San Pedro. A few years later, they were forced to abandon the building. In 1834, Abel bought the rundown warehouse and made extensive renovations: expanding it into a large quadrangle building with an office that contained comfortable accommodations for visitors and ample storerooms. In a matter of months, he had created a merchant monopoly that brought him an extraordinary amount of wealth.

The new warehouse also provided a service to rancheros who could now store their load of hides without needing to be in San Pedro on the exact day of a ship's arrival. For a commission, Abel also offered to do their trading for them, even delivering their purchases to their ranchos, using his own carts. Señoras and señoritas could still enjoy their visits to the warehouse's storefront to socialize and browse among an attractive array of select merchandise.

There was no stopping the shrewd businessman. After establishing the store and warehouse, Abel went into the lumber business. His agents in the north purchased cut timber and shipped it to his San Pedro warehouse where he would trade the building supplies to settlers in the comparatively treeless Southern California for hides and tallow, some cash, or liquor. The lumber business also flourished. Long before the Gold Rush, Abel had acquired the largest cash fortune in California.

In 1836, Abel was elected Sindico of the Ayuntamiento of Los Angeles. In this capacity, he performed the duties of a lawyer and fiscal agent for the town council to protect the interests of the Pueblo. He had no training as a lawyer. Three years later, a committee was appointed to draft a map of the city and its jurisdictions. Abel, who was still the town's lawyer and fiscal agent, offered his services as its surveyor. From this vantage point, he now had access to proprietary information about property and property owners, who were well-off and who might need a loan. He became a one-man lending institution, offering generous sums of money to property owners desperate to keep their land.

Abel made a lot of enemies from those loans. Without fully

understanding what they were signing, property owners agreed to payment schedules and interest rates that were impossible to pay. When they fell behind, he was quick to foreclose on the mortgages, seizing their land or any valuable property.

Abel also made enemies with other merchants. Around 1835, they repeatedly accused him of smuggling, bringing in goods without paying the import duties. The practice was widespread and usually condoned. Abel was less cautious, and it nearly cost him his life.

In the summer of 1835, he sold a barrel of wine to William Day who later returned and drunkenly complained that the wine was no good. Abel got angry, denied the accusation, and tried to throw William out of his store. William drew a knife and lunged at Abel, stabbing him in his hand, shoulder, and mouth, severely cutting his tongue. Angered by the accusation and attack, Abel took revenge. His assailant was found guilty and sentenced to five years of penal servitude and labor on public works. The wound to his mouth and tongue left him with disfiguring scars and a permanent speech impediment.

The smuggling charges and surprise inspections continued, but nothing was ever proven. All smuggling accusations ceased when Abel received a commission as a Customs Administrator.

In 1839, Abel's relationship with his partner got personal. A hostile Indian raid on Don Juan Bandini's San Diego home destroyed everything, all his property, and livestock. Believing his family would be safer living in Los Angeles, he applied to Governor Alvarado for land near El Pueblo de Los Angeles. The governor granted him the 40,500-acre Rancho Jurupa, near the San Gabriel Mission where he was also appointed the secular administrator. Abel was offered living accommodations in the Bandini home, which he accepted.

On June 22, 1841, 43-year-old Abel Stearns married Don Juan's 14-year-old daughter, Arcadia. In her later years, she became a powerful influence in Los Angeles through her philanthropic work, as well as being the "Godmother of Santa Monica."

The newlyweds took up residence at Abel's El Palacio, the enormous adobe he built on his first property acquisition in downtown Los Angeles. With her flair for style and entertaining, likely supported by her mother's own talent, Arcadia transformed their home into the social center of Los Angeles, drawing Abel into that unfamiliar world.

The following year, he purchased the 20,000-acre Rancho Los Alamitos as a summer home for his wife. It's interesting that while his Mexican citizenship entitled him to receive land grants, Abel preferred to pay cash.

Wealth assumes knowledge, power, and influence. In late 1842, Naval Commodore Thomas Catsby Jones contacted Abel about an urgent matter he feared might lead to war between Mexico and the United States. Acting on his own false conclusions, Jones captured the Port of Monterey, believing he was protecting it from the British.

Realizing his mistake, he could not apologize enough — to the current outgoing governor and the incoming one. When Jones heard that the newly-appointed Governor Micheltorena would be stopping in Los Angeles on his way to Monterey, he asked Abel to intervene as his diplomatic liaison. He readily agreed to assist in the matter. The Governor accepted Jones's apology.

Thomas Larkin likely recommended that Jones contact Abel. As equally independent and prosperous merchants, Thomas and Abel kept each other well-informed about the economic and political developments in Monterey and Los Angeles. As U.S. consul, Larkin appointed Abel his confidential agent for the United States government in Southern California. "From various circumstances," wrote Larkin, "I consider it of the greatest importance to me to have a confidential correspondent in your place of residence, one with whom I can rely on in the conducting and negotiating of my business."

Abel would not receive a salary, but Larkin said that he believed his interests could "be advanced at some future day not far distant; therefore the end may justify the means, at least in the result. You must only look for recompense and an extended knowledge of affairs." He told Abel not to let anyone know of his new position.

Abel agreed with Larkin that California's peaceful annexation by the United States would be in everyone's best interest. But, accepting this new position placed him in a very awkward position. American by birth, he was now a naturalized citizen of Mexico and serving as sub-prefect of Los Angeles under the Mexican government. Should that government hear of his covert activities, his life would be ruined.

At the Constitutional Convention, Abel was appointed to the committee to report the ways and means of defraying the expenses of the state government. He presented the committee's report as follows. That property tax would later prove to be his undoing.

(September 25) The undersigned, a member of the Committee, finds great difficulty in organizing the "ways and means" best adapted to the present peculiar and unprecedented circumstances in which the State is placed, but would recommend as the most eligible plan, that the Legislature be empowered to raise the proper revenue for defraying the State expenses by levying an Income Land Property Tax, which shall not exceed one quarter per cent; as likewise a Poll Tax, which shall be left to the Legislature to decide upon, both in relation to the amount as well as the manner of carrying out the same. A. STEARNS

After the Convention, Abel returned to Los Angeles and served as temporary alcalde until a mayor could be elected. The following year he was elected a state assemblyman.

In 1852, Abel suffered a devastating personal loss with the death of his longtime friend and confidant, Hugo Reid. Abel met Hugo in 1832 when the two bachelors rented rooms in Nathaniel Pryor's boarding house. Hugo was on vacation, visiting Los Angeles for the first time while Abel had been living there a year. The two men had much in common: both going to sea at an early age after suffering a personal tragedy, residing for some time in Mexico where they absorbed the language and culture so well they were often mistaken for locals. They both saw California as their land of opportunity.

While Abel had a relentless ambition to succeed, Hugo knew considerably more about finances and accounting. He shared these details in the many letters he and Abel exchanged over the years, each asking and offering advice on an array of business and personal matters.

Is it possible that following Hugo's death, Abel did not want anyone to know he had a "secret partner" who had been advising him all those years? Did he think his only recourse was to make his own financial decisions instead of trusting someone else? If this is true, it proved to be his tipping point. From the late 1850s through the early 1860s, Abel continued to acquire several more ranchos, mostly through foreclosure of defaulted loans, until he was the owner of the largest land empire in California, over 200,000 acres. But, why?

Six years later, Thomas Larkin died unexpectedly from a fever he contracted while visiting the gold mining town of Colusa. They had been close friends for nearly 30 years. Who else was left for Abel to confide in now that he had lost his two closest friends?

In 1860, he was elected supervisor for Los Angeles County, and later a member of the Los Angeles City Council. Note how his political career is moving backward, from representing the town at the state level to being a member of the city's primary governing body.

Abel may have succeeded in beating out all human rivals, but Mother Nature dealt him a blow that knocked him to his knees. The widespread drought of 1863-64 killed more than 50,000 of his cattle and nearly bankrupted him. He was unable to meet the tax obligations on his properties and faced a lawsuit from the County of Los Angeles.

In 1865, to pay a $20,000 debt, Abel was forced to sell the summer home he built for his wife at Rancho Los Alamitos. Eventually, more land was taken over by his debt collectors. A newspaper article describing Abel's ironic fate appeared in March 1867.

> A California misfortune. The many friends of Don Abel Stearns will learn with regret of his pecuniary misfortunes. A few years since he owned 40,000 head of cattle and refused $30,000 in coin for 1,000 head offered him by a San Francisco butcher; he did not need the money and did not sell. The drought killed off his cattle by thousands upon thousands, and today his property has to be sacrificed to pay his debts.

How many of those former landowners he forced into foreclosure took some small pleasure in reading about his fate?

Enter Alfred Robinson, an old acquaintance and business associate who saw an opportunity to benefit from Abel's misfortunes. Robinson would help Abel sell his existing ranchos and earn a tidy profit in the process. Robinson and four partners formed the Robinson Trust, which later became a prosperous real estate firm.

On May 25, 1868, Abel signed over to the Robinson Trust the deeds to more than 175,000 acres of his property. In exchange, the Robinson Trust agreed to give him $50,000 cash up front, market and sell his properties, and pay him $1.50 for every acre of land sold, in addition to one-eighth interest in the firm.

Everyone agreed to the terms. But, after completing the deal, Abel continued to act as if he still owned all the land. He rented acreage for grazing, even permitting sheep who ate the grass down to its roots, leaving the land barren. He made arrangements on his own with prospective buyers without consulting Alfred Robinson.

On August 23, 1871, 73-year-old Abel died unexpectedly while staying at the Grand Hotel in San Francisco. His obituary does not mention the cause of death. It was written in a very matter-of-fact tone, mainly referencing his business accomplishments and later financial downturn. What's missing is any praise for the man's character, or any good works he accomplished, or how much family and friends will miss him. But at one time, for a very long time, he was the wealthiest man in California.

4

Hugo Reid

Hugo was born on April 18, 1811, in Cardross Scotland, across the bay from Glasgow. A fellow Scotsman insisted that a failed romance provoked 18-year-old Hugo to abandon his studies at Cambridge and take up the life of a merchant seaman.

Three years later, Hugo was living in Hermosillo Sonora, Mexico's most northwest state. As the representative of Henry Dalton's trading company, Hugo became rich selling merchandise to prosperous gold miners, but he was exhausted. He preferred a leisurely life, one filled with relaxation, music, and books. A fellow Scotsman, about to sail up the California Coast, invited Hugo along as a round-trip passenger. He accepted.

Hugo disembarked in San Pedro where he would have one week until the ship returned. He rode on horseback to El Pueblo de Los Angeles where he spent the entire week getting to know the area and its hospitable residents. Los Angeles, he believed, could offer him the life of leisure he was seeking.

Two years later, Hugo returned to El Pueblo de Los Angeles where he hoped to finally settle down. He formed a trading company with Jacob Leese in a large adobe on the Plaza. The storefront offered food, fabrics, furniture, shoes, dress patterns, ready-made clothing, even window glass, carpeting, and hardware.

Hugo enjoyed helping the customers carry their packages to their waiting carriages or ox carts. The day he helped doña Eulalia Perez, majordomo for the nearby Mission San Gabriel, began a new chapter in his life. Waiting in the ox cart was the most beautiful Indian woman Hugo had ever seen. Her name was Victoria. Hugo was so smitten by Victoria that he remembered very little from that first meeting except that doña Eulalia invited him to come to her home some afternoon for tea.

Hugo enjoyed many afternoon teas at doña Eulalia's home in conversation with Victoria. She told him stories about her ancestors, chieftains of the proud and independent Gabrielenos Indians, "converted" by the Padres to a life of servitude. Hugo also learned that Victoria was a wife and mother. Whatever his feelings for her, those afternoon visits were all he could ever enjoy with her.

Hugo's plan to settle down in El Pueblo de Los Angeles fell apart. Unrequited love, a dissolved business partnership, and being framed for a serious crime were too much for the young romantic. He returned to Hermosillo and opened a school for boys, determined to dedicate his life to its success. However, when he received a letter that Victoria's husband had died from smallpox, Hugo returned to El Pueblo de Los Angeles, and never looked back. Victoria accepted his marriage proposal.

Everyone knew that 26-year-old Hugo was in love with 35-year-old Victoria, that nothing they could say would persuade him that this union was not a good one for either of them. Yet,

Hugo's marriage to Victoria would provide him his only legacy, after all he had gained—and lost.

The marriage customs of 1837 required that Hugo be baptized a Catholic, produce four character witnesses who have known him for a long time and submit to an exhaustive marriage investigation. He did all this willingly. He also applied for Mexican citizenship. Regardless of the disapproval of the romance between Hugo and Victoria, everyone for miles around attended the wedding fiesta and the pageant.

Doña Eulalia raised Victoria from a child and educated her well. She was also responsible for Victoria regaining her Gabrieleno Indian heritage, thus distinguishing her as one of a handful of members of her race ever to own land in Alta California under a Mexican grant. Victoria claimed title to two ranchos: the 13,300-acre Santa Anita and La Huerta del Cuati, which yielded a substantial income from cattle, sheep, grapevines, and short crops. With consistent care and management, Victoria's ranchos would provide a comfortable living for Hugo, Victoria, and their children. Hugo underestimated what was required to maintain Rancho Santa Anita. His first mistake was moving his family into the more-populated San Gabriel where he built a home near the San Gabriel Mission, naming it Uva Espina.

With his new status as a man of property, Don Hugo was elected to his first public office, the city council.

He adopted Victoria's three children and fathered three more. Convincing himself that owning so much productive land meant he did not need to work, Don Hugo devoted his time to educating his wife and children. The children thrived under his teaching, but Dona Victoria resisted, preferring they all be outdoors.

She was concerned that spending too much time indoors would

ruin the children's health. Hugo had recently developed a chronic complaint of the chest, which, she was sure, was caused by his sedentary, indoor habits. He frequently postponed trips into town because of bad weather. A slight rainfall would have him bedridden for several days while the heat of the San Gabriel sun exhausted him.

In May 1839, two claims were filed against Rancho Santa Anita, disrupting Hugo's plan to be an absentee landlord. When the local authorities didn't respond to his letters, he wrote directly to Governor Alvarado, outlining in precise detail his plans for improving the property. The governor accepted his claim. Hugo had work to do.

At Rancho Santa Anita he built a house out of stone, high on a hill, with stone steps leading down to a small boat landing on the lake. The new home, shaded by cottonwoods and willow trees, overlooked the entire San Gabriel Valley. Hugo reduced the number of grazing cattle and planted fruit trees, a vegetable garden, more grape vines, and wheat. In his desperation to save the property, Hugo had not considered how much year-round labor was now required to maintain the improved rancho. Wheat and corn needed to be sown in December and harvested from July through September. The grape vineyards needed regular irrigating, the grapes needed harvesting at intervals and making wine after every harvest. The cattle roundup happened every April. Animals were doctored, dehorned and branded. Hugo's effort to provide for his family made Victoria very happy.

Hugo and Abel Stearns lived a few miles apart and saw each other often. They also kept in touch with letter-writing, asking the advice of each other on business or personal matters, commenting on local gossip, even confiding on personal issues. The

Scotsman and the American met in 1832 when they were each renting rooms in Nathaniel Pryor's boarding house. Both had lived in Mexico for a long time, absorbing the language and culture through their work as representatives of different trading companies. Both had dreams of one-day owning land and being very rich. When Hugo confided to Abel that he was feeling trapped by all the work at the rancho and restless for the open seas, Abel told him about the 92-ton Mexican schooner, *Esmeralda*, that was for sale at a low price.

Despite his family's pleas, Hugo bought the *Esmeralda* in 1842, eager to sail the high seas once more, now as a merchant sea captain and return a prosperous one. He returned six months later, very homesick, and having lost a great deal of money. In his absence, the livestock and crops at Rancho San Anita had fallen into a state of neglect. Hugo needed money right away. Again, he set sail on the *Esmeralda*, aware that in his absence the Rancho would further deteriorate.

He traveled to the Orient, another unsuccessful and costly voyage. When he returned, he confided to Abel that he was now in severe debt. He thought his only option was to sell some of Victoria's property. Would it be the Rancho that she loved so dearly or the thriving vineyard that had produced so many bottles of delicious wine?

The neighboring Gabrielenos were devoted to Hugo for the generosity and compassion he showed them. Unaware of his financial difficulties, they elected him to their highest public office, justice of the peace. Mothers wanted their children baptized by him instead of the padre. But Hugo had done all he could to improve their lives. The Mission Indians rebelled and raided outlying ranchos. Hugo and Victoria tried to protect both the Mission and the Indians. In February 1846, Hugo wrote a petition and sent it to Governor Pio Pico. It was signed by 140 Gabrielenos.

The petition listed numerous grievances against the padres and majordomos. It respectfully requested that the governor abolish ecclesiastical control and transform the mission into a pueblo. The request was denied because of the Mission's massive debt. This further frustrated the Indians who resumed their raids.

Mission leaders reappointed Hugo justice of the peace and administrator of mission affairs. On June 8, 1846, Hugo announced what he believed was a mutually-beneficial solution. He would purchase Mission San Gabriel.

The initial transaction did not go through. Colonel John Fremont, claiming he was acting on behalf of the United States government, arrived and dispossessed them before the term of payment was fixed. However, a few months later, when Pio Pico was appointed interim governor, he distributed mission property among his friends. He gave Hugo the title to Mission San Gabriel lands. Hugo then sold Victoria's 13,300-acre Rancho Santa Anita to his longtime friend and former employer, Henry Dalton—for a mere $2,700.

The ranchers wanted the Indian raids to stop. U.S. military forces launched ruthless campaigns against the Indians. On February 24, 1848, the Los Angeles city council sent an official communication to (future delegate) Stephen Foster, alcalde of the city of Los Angeles. "The public peace requires that the Indian ranch areas in the vicinity of the Pueblo be broken up and removed to a greater distance from the town. You are therefore requested to cause the removal, or breakage up, on or before the night of the twenty-sixth ..."

The order gave the spirited Gabrielenos only two days to break up their homes. They refused to comply with such an unjust order without force.

The chaos in Hugo's life persisted. While Alvarado was governor when Commodore Jones "captured" Monterey, he was soon replaced by Micheltorena, who was more favorable to the Americans, which proved to be his undoing. Governor Micheltorena was forced into exile and replaced by Pio Pico. At the start of the U.S. military forces moving south in 1846, Pico fled across the border into Mexico, supposedly to ask the government for more troops.

Returning alone to California, he showed up unannounced at Hugo's home seeking refuge. There was a rumor that Pico was returning to regain his governorship. Colonel Stevenson had two search parties of New York Volunteers out looking for Pico. Would Hugo be implicated for harboring a fugitive?

Pico dragged Hugo deeper into his fiasco. He wanted him to negotiate with Colonel Stevenson for his protection. Did Hugo feel obligated to repay a debt? Wasn't it Pico who had granted him all that mission land? Hugo succeeded in obtaining a safe-conduct note from Colonel Stevenson that came with conditions. Pico must not interfere in any civil or military matters, a tragic consequence for Hugo.

Land grants bearing Pico's signature were invalidated. Hugo lost ownership of Mission San Gabriel. He was so deep in debt that it was impossible to manage even the small Huerta del Cuati and Uva Espina properties. Desperate for money and willing to do *anything*, the news of gold at Sutter's Mill pulled him away from his family to chase after another foolish scheme.

In June 1849, while Hugo was searching for gold, Maria Ygnacia, doña Victoria's beautiful daughter, died from smallpox.

Known as the "flower of San Gabriel," Maria Ygnacia was the belle of the ball at every party and the light of her mother's life. In her agonizing grief, Victoria convinced herself that Hugo had murdered her daughter by having her stay indoors so much to study.

In one of only two letters she wrote in her entire life, Victoria told Abel Stearns, "It is a waste of life to learn from books. My husband kept her too long indoors, to read in English and French and do silly sums. Away from the sun, she grew pale and weak, unable to fight the dreadful disease. It is because of Don Hugo and his learning that she died." Hugo left the mines and headed home as soon as he heard that Maria Ygnacia was ill. He did not arrive until after her funeral where he was confronted by his wife's hatred.

Victoria withdrew deeper into her grief and anger. Hugo returned to the mines, fooling himself into believing he would find enough gold to clear his debts, restore his financial status, and regain Victoria's love.

A couple of months later, Hugo wrote to Abel from Monterey, pleading with him to stay away from the mines. They were loaded with plenty of goods as well as vagabonds, assassins, lynching parties, and fatal diseases.

> The mines I could not stand, but came out on foot to Fort Sutter. San Francisco nearly killed me with a complaint of the chest from which I am only now recovering, being still very hoarse. There I could procure no passage by water and no horses; so after remaining six weeks, I started, sick as I was, on foot and walked down here [to Monterey] in five days. ...[I met up with my Scotch friend] McKinley, having no great assistant and doing all the business of the place, made me an offer better than gold digging. I have accepted. I am also about to advertise my home in San Gabriel, to let or lease. ...There is

no place like Los Angeles yet, but circumstances oblige me to remain here, I suppose a couple years.

McKinley's store was well-stocked with most everything a miner needed. Hugo quickly made a fortune, selling all sorts of supplies and receiving a substantial share in the profits, but he was sickly. The hardships he had suffered in the mines and the long walk with his son Felipe from San Francisco to Monterey aggravated his chronic chest complaint. Meanwhile, in the Los Angeles District, the committee nominating delegates to the Constitutional Convention elected Hugo. While he was likely in Monterey at the start of the Convention, he didn't arrive in Colton Hall until the afternoon of September 5 with the other Los Angeles delegates.

Hugo was in attendance throughout the entire Convention. He served on the census committee and the boundary committee. While he did not participate in any discussions or debates, he voted regularly.

When the Convention adjourned for the last time, Hugo returned to working full-time in McKinley's store. He was too late. There was insurmountable debt, and little money left in reserve. Neither partner's private resources were sufficiently adequate to carry the business until conditions improved.

At the end of 1850, McKinley & Reid went out of business. Financially, Hugo was back where he had started, before the Gold Rush. Physically, he had aged several years and was in much worse health. There were no more financial prospects for him in Monterey, or anywhere else, for that matter. There was nothing left for him to do but return to what remained of his home—and to a wife who hated him.

Before they were married, Hugo had promised Victoria that

someday he would vindicate her people through his pen. Over the years, he had acquired a deep understanding of the Gabrieleno Indian nature, his sense of justice outraged again and again. It was time to fulfill that promise.

Victoria agreed to help him in every way possible, searching her memory and encouraging her people to contribute their own memories. With her loving support, Hugo started work on the Indian essays, a series of 22 letters that would become his most enduring legacy.

Hugo and Victoria also interviewed the few Indians who could remember the ancient "court language" and generally forgotten customs and beliefs. For several weeks, Hugo collected subject matter for the essays. Then one day, he just vanished from San Gabriel, without telling Victoria or anyone else, even his confidant Abel Stearns, where he was going.

For several months, no one had any news of Hugo or knew what to say to Victoria to console her. Then one day, he reappeared, saying in a subdued voice that he had been in retreat. He had completed the Indian essays, and they were ready for publication.

William Grant, the editor of the new Los Angeles Star, accepted them without hesitation. He also hired Hugo as the paper's San Gabriel correspondent, offering him a fair salary. In the February 21, 1852, issue, Grant announced that he had received "a series of articles upon the manners, customs, etc. of the Indians, from the pen of Hugo Reid, a gentleman well conversant with the subject of which he treats."

Hugo began the essays with a description of the Indians' language, customs, religion, and legends. He concluded with a poignant account of current conditions and a plea to end the

The Delegates of 1849

"legislative oppression." The essays attained national significance, serving as the basis for U.S. Indian agent Benito Wilson's humane report to Washington.

Hugo's next project was compiling a vocabulary and complete language manual for the Southern California tribes. He never finished.

On December 12, 1852, Hugo died at the age of 41 after suffering for years from tuberculosis.

In October 1937, a six-foot-tall sculpture by Preston Prescott titled "Hugo Reid Family" was dedicated in Arcadia Park. The WPA federal project commemorated the first permanent home in Arcadia and is now a historical landmark.

5

Stephen Clark Foster

Stephen was born on December 17, 1820, in East Machias Maine. His fourth great-grandfather emigrated from Exeter England to Ipswich Massachusetts before 1652. When 20-year-old Stephen graduated from Yale College in 1840, he did not return to the family's home place but set off to find his own home.

He taught school in Virginia and Alabama for a few years, then traveled to New Orleans where he attended lectures at the Louisiana Medical College. His newly-acquired knowledge enabled him to briefly practice medicine the following year in Jackson County Missouri.

Stephen left Missouri as the business partner of an Irish schoolmaster bound for Santa Fe New Mexico. By the time they reached Santa Fe the partnership had dissolved. While working as a store clerk, he heard that the Mormon Battalion of Iowa Volunteers were on their way to California to fight in the Mexican-American War. They needed an interpreter and Stephen was fluent in Spanish. He won the appointment and was commissioned as a captain, a rank that paid $75 a month plus rations. He was required to provide his own uniform, firearms, and mount. While he was an accomplished horseman, a mule suited his purpose just fine.

The Battalion endured one physical hardship after another on the 830-mile march. The worst deprivation was the short rations. The unit started out with provisions for 60 days but did not arrive in San Diego until 110 days later in January 1847. Stephen was headquartered in Los Angeles when the war ended in June 1847. At last, he had found his forever home.

In January 1848, Military Governor Mason appointed him alcalde of Los Angeles. At the July 4th celebration, he read the Declaration of Independence in Spanish to the gratitude of the local citizens.

On August 5, 1848, 28-year-old Stephen married the 33-year-old widow, María Merced Lugo, joining a prominent Los Angeles family. The Fosters would have five children. Maria and the children liked living at their country home in San Antonio on the San Gabriel River. Stephen preferred the active city life where he participated in civic affairs, as a private citizen and an elected official.

In May 1849, his position as alcalde was replaced by a city council. Around this time, he received Governor Riley's Proclamation calling for the election of delegates to a constitutional convention in Monterey. He also received a private letter from Henry W. Halleck, captain of engineers, United States Army, and secretary of state, informing him that it was of utmost importance that Southern California was adequately represented at the Convention. Henry asked Stephen to use his influence in persuading the people of Los Angeles to hold an election.

What was at stake was the Missouri Compromise Line of 1820, that if extended horizontally across California, would divide the state in two, with slavery likely being introduced in the southern portion. As a further inducement to the delegates from San Diego, Los Angeles, Santa Barbara, and San Luis Obispo to attend the Convention, as well as facilitate their timely arrival, the U.S. propeller ship *Edith* was commissioned to transport them to Monterey.

Stephen took Governor Riley's request very seriously. At his own expense, he posted notices in all the precincts, doing everything possible to encourage the people to vote for the men who would best represent them. Only one delegate election was held in Los Angeles, during a feast and fandango at the home of a prominent Angeleno. There was no electioneering, party nominations, or dissent. Forty-eight votes were tallied, electing Stephen as one of the delegates to represent his new home of Los Angeles.

He wrote in his memoir,

> I knew no one in Monterey, and as we had no idea where the money was to come from to pay our expenses, I was at first dubious about going, hardly considering the honor to be acquired. We had no news of the promised steamer, the Edith (lost off Point Conception): so, on August 20, 1849, Stearns, Dominguez, Carrillo and I, ... started from Los Angeles together, on horseback, for Monterey [a distance of three hundred miles]. Hugo Reid, a native of Scotland, was already in Monterey and completed the full delegation.
>
> The common mode of making long journeys here then was to take four or five horses to each rider. The loose horses were driven along, and whenever any horse showed signs of fatigue, a fresh horse was caught, the saddle was shifted, and the tired horse turned into the band, and the rate of traveling was sixty or seventy miles a day. The scarcity of servants, caused by the gold fever, was the reason that the two Californians and myself started each with one horse. Don Abel Stearns, as "El Rico" (the rich man) of the delegation, took along a vaquero, with six spare horses; but since, if he rode California fashion, he would have to go alone, he concluded to jog along with the

rest. There were no hotels from San Diego to Monterey then, and each night we lodged at some private house gratis. No greater insult could have been offered to a ranchero than to offer to pay for one's accommodation.

At the Convention,

Sept. 5. Mr. Foster ... was opposed at present to entering into a State Government. ...

Mr. Foster, although acting under instructions similar to those of his colleague did not believe that a majority of his constituents wished a separation [by dividing the state in two]. There was no doubt they desired a Territorial Government, but he believed they would prefer to bear their share of the burden of a State Government rather than divide the country.

Following the Convention, Stephen would spend the next several years in public office. In 1850, he was elected to the Los Angeles Common Council, serving for one year. In 1851, he was elected state senator from Southern California, serving for two years.

In 1853, he was appointed to the first public school board, the start of today's Board of Education.

From 1854-1855, he served as mayor of the City of Los Angeles, and authorized construction of the first public school at Spring and 2nd Streets.

Los Angeles at that time was known as the toughest frontier town in America. The surrounding territory was overrun by bandits driven from the gold mines south into the cattle ranching counties. Numerous gamblers and criminals also drifted into the city to escape the San Francisco vigilantes.

Mayor Foster, like most of the city's prominent citizens, was a member of the local vigilance committee and of the Los Angeles Rangers, the mounted body of volunteer police.

Late in 1854, Dave Brown murdered his friend, Pinckney Clifford, without provocation. He was tried before Judge Hayes, found guilty, and sentenced to hang on the same date that a Mexican was to hang for another murder. The Mexican was hanged on the appointed day and time, but Brown's American lawyers secured for him a stay of execution. The fact that one guilty criminal was hanged while the other equally guilty one was reprieved through high legal talent infuriated the citizens of Los Angeles into demanding that the law be ignored and Brown lynched on the spot.

Mayor Foster had promised the people at the time of the capture that justice would be served. He kept his word. On January 13, the day following the Mexican's execution, he resigned as mayor. As a private citizen, he led the mob which forced the jail, dragged Brown out across Spring Street and hanged him on a corral gate opposite the old jail. Stephen was now out of a job.

Two weeks later, on January 25, 1855, the people held a special election and returned Stephen as mayor for the remainder of his regular term. He was also appointed the superintendent of schools.

He was re-elected mayor in 1856, resigning a few months later to serve as executor for the large estate of his brother-in-law, Colonel Isaac Williams. In 1856, 1858 and 1859 he was elected to the Los Angeles County Board of Supervisors.

After he retired from public life, Stephen continued living in town while his family lived at San Antonio. Somewhat infirm in his later years, he was often seen walking on the streets through Los Angeles. His familiarity with the old Spanish archives and Pueblo land titles earned him a small stipend from title searchers.

He died on January 28, 1898, at the age of 78 and was buried at New Calvary Catholic Cemetery in Los Angeles.

> *"Above all, the kindly, sympathetic spirit towards the Spanish-speaking Californians and others of the olden times which pervaded all that [Stephen] wrote or said concerning them, is worthy of unreserved commendation and admiration."*

PART II

Monterey District

6

Thomas Oliver Larkin

Thomas was no doubt a proud husband and father when he returned to the East in 1850 with his wife and children. They represented success as much as the wealth and prestige he had acquired in California.

Thomas was born on September 16, 1802, in Charlestown Massachusetts. He was five years old when his father died, 11 years old when his mother remarried and 15 years old when she died. Whether it was his decision or his stepfather's, he left home at that time, and attempted several occupations in several cities for several years before returning home, destitute and dejected.

When his older half-brother, Captain John Bautista Rogers Cooper, wrote that he was in desperate need of an efficient assistant with his trading business in Monterey California, 29-year-old Thomas had no idea that joining him would transform his life so dramatically. He sailed from Boston aboard the *Newcastle* in September 1831. The ship's seven-month course was around the Cape Horn at the tip of South America.

Also onboard was 24-year-old Rachel Hobson Holmes, sailing

to California to join her husband, a Danish seaman. Thomas and Rachel were close companions for those seven months, also traveling together from San Francisco to Monterey where they boarded at Captain Cooper's home for a short while. Rachel then went on to Santa Barbara where she gave birth to Thomas's daughter, who lived only six months. While in Santa Barbara, Rachel learned that her husband had died at sea the year before. Thomas and Rachel were soon married.

Captain Cooper arrived in California in 1823, opened a general merchandise store in 1826 and married Mariano Vallejo's sister, Encarnacion Vallejo, in 1827. His store served all the residents, from poor Indians to the elite Castro, Soberanes, and Osio families. Cooper and Thomas kept detailed accounts that reveal what a boon their trading store was to the local economy. Wages were sometimes paid "in cash," but more often entered as a credit against purchases. Cooper and Thomas mediated labor arrangements, paid the workers in cash or kind, and charged it to the employer's account—acting as a type of bank.

Thomas worked with his brother for about a year, until he had saved enough money to open a small store. Unlike his earlier failed attempts on the East Coast, every business venture he attempted in California was successful. From his store profits, Thomas built a double-geared flour mill, the first of its kind on the West Coast. He also invested in a sawmill in Santa Cruz that earned him a profit.

In 1835, Thomas built the first two-story house in California, a combination of New England and Spanish Colonial style that is known today as Monterey Colonial architecture. The ground floor served as the store and storeroom while the family lived upstairs. Future fellow-delegate, Mariano Vallejo, would build his home in Petaluma in the same style. Thomas also constructed the first wharf at Monterey Harbor and was commissioned to rebuild the Custom House.

Within six years, Thomas's commercial activities eclipsed those of his half-brother. He was in a good position to begin trading with Mexico, the United States, and other countries.

Thomas's prominence and political savvy enabled him to survive as a "foreigner" through the Mexican government's shifting administrations. He never applied for Mexican citizenship, preferring to renew his visa every year. As a non-citizen, he could not legally own land, but he was able to obtain land grants in his children's names. Thomas and Rachel became parents to seven more children, five surviving to adulthood.

On October 19, 1842, when U.S. Commodore Thomas Catesby Jones landed marines in Monterey to capture the town and keep it out of British hands, Thomas and William Hartnell acted quickly to downplay the calamity. They convinced the Commodore that there was no invasion and persuaded him to withdraw his troops as well as submit a written apology to the angry Mexican officials. (This is the same Jones who contacted Abel Stearns to assist him in apologizing to incoming Governor Micheltorena on his way up from Mexico.)

Word of Thomas's successful diplomatic efforts came to the attention of officials in Washington. In 1843, President John Tyler appointed him consul to Alta California.

Thomas's intense attention to detail served him well. His confidential transmittals to Washington provided elaborate descriptions of the country and its political state. He also commented on the political leanings of prominent citizens, many whom he had been talking with about the advantages of Alta California aligning with the United States.

In 1845, Thomas hired William Leidesdorff as his vice consul in San Francisco. The following year he received instructions from Secretary of State James Buchanan to begin working covertly to assure all concerned Californios that the United States would support any attempt at secession from Mexico. With Leidesdorff reporting to him on the state of affairs in Northern California, he discretely appointed Abel Stearns as his unofficial, and unpaid, vice-counsel to keep him informed of matters in Southern California.

With tensions increasing between the U.S. and Mexican governments, Thomas wrote to Washington, volunteering to go to Mexico City. He and General Mariano Vallejo, Mexico's official representative, had been in earnest discussion, hoping to arrange a peaceful annexation of Alta California that would keep it out of the impending conflict. Thomas's letter was en route when Congress declared war. The Bear Flag Revolt of June 1846 brought the fight to California.

Supposedly on a mapmaking expedition of California, John Fremont, Lieutenant of Engineers in the Army Topographical Service, actively encouraged settlers to rebel against Mexican rule. Acting on a rumor that the Mexican authorities were thinking of arresting all Americans, he responded—without authorization—by sending a party of men into Sonoma, where they seized the peaceful town, arrested General Vallejo, and declared California a Republic. Fremont did not consult with Thomas, the official U.S. representative, before waging his war.

The American military conquest of Alta California grew beyond Thomas's control. Fremont's California Battalion continued to expand as more and more settlers were coerced into joining the fight. Responding to the foreign invasion, the "enemy" Californios rebelled against the under-staffed California Battalion garrison troops and Navy forces.

Fearing for his family's safety, Thomas sent them to Yerba Buena (San Francisco) while he remained behind in Monterey. Learning that his daughter was very ill, he tried to ride unnoticed into San Francisco. Renegade Californios captured him and held him prisoner in Los Angeles. He was released four months later after the Treaty of Cahuenga was signed on January 13, 1847. His daughter died during his captivity.

In partnership with future fellow delegates Robert Semple and Mariano Vallejo, the three entrepreneurs established the city of Benicia. The location, 37 miles northwest along the north bank of the Carquinez Strait, rivaled Yerba Buena. Referred to as the best natural site for a commercial city, Benicia needed time and money to become established. San Francisco newspapers carried enthusiastic advertisements of lots for sale.

Robert and Mariano were pleased that Benicia was thriving and drawing attention away from San Francisco. Thomas, on the other hand, now saw Benicia's success as a threat to his profitable San Francisco investments. He had to choose. He severed his partnership with Robert and Mariano, little knowing their paths would cross again at the Constitutional Convention in Monterey. Without Thomas's substantial influence, Benicia would never surpass San Francisco. By the late 1840s, Thomas and his family had permanently settled in San Francisco and were there for the economic boom that followed.

The Larkins returned briefly to Monterey in 1849 where Thomas assisted Henry Halleck in directing the preparations for the Constitutional Convention and serving as a delegate. He and other prominent residents continuously hosted elaborate affairs in their homes where the delegates participated in lively discussions on the Convention's topic of the day. He also invited at least one delegate to his home every day for lunch and another for dinner throughout the six weeks of the Convention.

Thomas was present on the first day of the Convention and voted throughout but did not participate in any discussions or debates on the floor. What was the point? He'd already influenced the outcome of the debates at his dining table.

After the Constitutional Convention adjourned, 48-year-old Thomas was relieved of his duties as U.S. consul. Thanks to his San Francisco investments, he was also exceptionally wealthy, and could now relax and enjoy his life. In early 1850, he began construction of the first brick building in San Francisco on Stockton Street. Later that year, he took his family to New York so that his five surviving children could receive an East Coast education. While in New York, he read California newspapers and often wrote to them, describing how much he was looking forward to his return.

After returning to California, Thomas visited Colusa where he contracted typhoid fever and died on October 27, 1858, at the age of 56. For weeks, the newspapers printed heartfelt tributes about the man, his life and his legacy.

> The funeral of the late Thomas O. Larkin took place yesterday at noon. The California Pioneers at that hour assembled at the residence of the deceased and bore his remains to Trinity Chapel ... The procession numbered one hundred pioneers on foot and forty-three carriages ... Thus has departed from amongst us one of whom it may

be in truth said that "None knew him but to love him; none named him but to praise."

The talented sculptor, Thomas J. Donnelly, has exhibited to us a plaster cast of the face of the late Thomas O. Larkin. The likeness is a singularly striking one, ... The nicely chiseled mouth is particularly pleasing, reminding one of the beautiful expression which it always wore during the lifetime of the deceased.

He was emphatically the highest type of the American pioneer and the best exponent of our national interest on this coast during the eventful periods of this country's history up to 1849. He was our state's best pioneer. ... It is enough to say that in every respect he performed the duties of the office with honor to his country and to himself. Such services deserved and received, through the Secretary of State of the United States, "the thanks of the president for his attention for so many years to the cause of this country.

7

Pacificus Ord

Pacificus's father James was believed to be the illegitimate son of King George IV and Maria Fritzherbert. "[Young James] was thought to have been sent to Spain and then to America in the care of the Ord family. It was said that James Ord bore a striking resemblance to King George IV and that his Georgetown University tuition and fees were paid by the British Legation."

Born on October 16, 1816, in Cumberland Maryland, Pacificus would have 11 siblings. Three brothers would follow in their father's footsteps and enjoy prominent military careers while Pacificus instead became a miniature portrait artist. By age 26, he turned his attention to the study of law, which he practiced in New Orleans where he was admitted to the bar in 1844.

In 1848, the 32-year-old married 25-year-old Maria Louisa Pogue. The following year they came to Monterey on the *California*, the first steamship to come around Cape Horn. Pacificus set up his law practice but it is unknown how successful he was. Two of their children would survive to adulthood.

Brother Edward, a West Point graduate, had arrived in California the previous year aboard the USS *Lexington* and was stationed at the Monterey Presidio where brother James was the military surgeon. Fort Ord in Seaside was named after Major General Edward Ord. Siblings Robert, William, and Georgianna also came to California. After the Mexican-American War, and until the Civil War when he further distinguished himself, Edward was a surveyor and charter member of the Society of California Pioneers. James married Angustias de la Guerra, Pablo de la Guerra's sister.

In 1849, Pacificus suspended his law practice to serve as a delegate to the Constitutional Convention. The following are samples of Pacificus's rational comments during the Convention.

September 11. Mr. Ord submitted the following amendment as an additional section.
Sec. 17. The right of the people to be secure in their persons, houses, papers, and effects against unreasonable seizures and searches, shall not be violated; and no warrant shall issue but on probable cause, supported by oath or affirmation, particularly describing the place to be searched, and the papers and things to be seized.

September 25. The first section of the report of the Committee being under consideration, Mr. Ord offered a substitute for the whole report, which was read.
Mr. Ord said he offered this substitute because he thought the judicial system proposed by the Committee was unsuited to the wants and the condition of the people of California. His first objection was that it was too complicated. There were four tribunals proposed by the Committee: 1st, the Supreme Court; 2d,

the Circuit Court; 3d, the County Court; 4th, the Magistrates' Court. He regarded that as a serious objection. Another objection: He thought the system an expensive one; that it would be found, when put in practice, extremely costly. A third objection was that it would give rise to delays in the administration of justice—delays which he was sure every citizen of California was anxious to avoid.

In 1852, his wife Maria died. In 1855, he was appointed U.S. attorney for the Southern District of California and served until 1859, filing appeals on behalf of the United States against Mexican landowners who had trusted the terms of the [Peace] Treaty of Guadalupe Hidalgo that they could hold onto their former Mexican rancho lands.

In 1862, 46-year-old Pacificus married Helen Rebecca Masterson in San Francisco. They traveled throughout Europe for several years until her death. He returned to the East Coast, and in 1873, 57-year-old Pacificus married the 57-year-old widow, Ann Galilee in Manhattan New York. She died 10 years later while the couple was touring England. Pacificus died on May 11, 1900, in Washington, D.C. at the age of 84.

8

Lewis Dent

The Dent family in America can be traced to the 1660s. Among them are several distinguished military men, including Lewis's father and two older brothers whose ranks respectively were Colonel, Captain and Brigadier General. Captain John, was a close personal friend of Ulysses Simpson Grant during their early military days and Brigadier General Frederick, a West Point graduate, was Grant's aide-de-camp during the Civil War. His youngest sister Julia married the future U.S. President in 1848. Lewis's son would graduate from Annapolis.

Yet, Lewis cannot claim any distinguishing notoriety. Photographs are available of Lewis's father and brothers, looking proud in their military uniforms; but there are no public images of Lewis. It's as if he spent his life on the outside looking in, despite a lifetime of unrelenting effort.

Lewis was born in St. Louis Missouri on March 3, 1823. The earliest available records about him are letters he wrote to the St. Louis [Weekly] Reveille concerning his time as a non-Mormon, nonmilitary assistant paymaster clerk to the paymaster of the Mormon Battalion during their long and arduous march to San Diego.

After being discharged in 1847 from his service with the U.S. Army and the U.S. Mormon Battalion, Lewis moved to Monterey where he wrote in 1848,

> ... My [law] office is in the dwelling house of Gen. Alvarado, former governor of the territory under the Mexican supremacy. [Regarding the local California citizens,] they do not resemble us in a single particular. ... They are in short power opposites in every respect. ... Our laws must be carefully introduced among them, and we must lead them to appreciate our most enlightened code and adopt our better customs. ... The people have a great predilection for revolution. ... At present the country is quiet, but I do not imagine it will long continue so ... I should believe a military despotism to be the form of government most suited to their condition.

It's unknown how Lewis came to be a delegate representing Monterey at the Constitutional Convention. He favored dueling.

September 27: No clause that you can introduce in the Constitution will prevent a man from fighting a duel if it be in defense of his honor. There are few men who will not risk their lives when their honor is at stake. If a man be forbidden to hold office because he has too much respect for his honor, we place him in a degraded position. It may be said that it is a false sense of honor, but there may be circumstances in every man's life to induce him, if he possess one particle of manliness or one principle of liberty, to defend his honor at the risk of his life. If we had in the Constitution of the United States a clause like this, Hamilton, Randolph, Jackson, Clay, and Benton would have been dropped from the role of American statesmen. Their eminent services would not have been known to the public. For this reason, I am in favor of striking out this clause from the Constitution, and I sincerely hope that other members will sustain me.

In early November 1849, William Knight was killed in a shootout. His river crossing, Knights Ferry, traversed the Stanislaus River from Stockton to the southern mines, earning him about $500 a day. For reasons unknown, Lewis and his brother John became the new owners of Knights Ferry.

The following year they built the Knights Ferry House, a restaurant and boarding house. The year after that, brother George and his wife joined them. Lewis was doing quite well for himself in the trading business. In 1853, David Locke, in partnership with the Dent brothers, built the first dam on the Stanislaus River.

Captain Ulysses S. Grant was stationed on the West Coast in Eureka and visited Knights Ferry three times between 1852 and 1854. Is it possible that during these visits he formed opinions about the three Dent brothers that would later influence his relationships with them as President?

In 1854, a bridge was built across the Stanislaus River that put the ferry out of business but provided an opportunity for the Dent brothers and David Locke to erect a grist mill and a sawmill.

In December 1855, 32-year-old Lewis married 16-year-old Anna Elizabeth Bain, a native of Mississippi.

In 1856, the town of Knights Ferry was laid out on the north bank of the Stanislaus River. Some referred to it as Dentville, since by now the three Dent brothers and their families lived there. The town grew and prospered. Brother George became postmaster, brother John became the Indian agent and ran the trading post with Lewis.

In 1858, Lewis left Dentville and with his family moved 40 miles away to Stockton where he formed a law partnership with the former editor of the San Joaquin Republican.

Two years later, Judge Lewis Dent was elected a trustee of the Stockton Insane Asylum.

After the Civil War, Lewis moved his family to his wife's home state of Mississippi. He rented plantations in Mississippi and Louisiana where he raised cotton.

On March 4, 1869, his brother-in-law, Ulysses, was sworn in as the 18th President of the United States. President Grant gave appointments to Lewis's three brothers but refused to have anything to do with him. The rest of Lewis's life story can best be told through the following newspaper excerpts.

> July 8, 1869 In Mississippi the Republicans have called on Louis Dent to become their candidate for governor and Dent accepts. He is a brother-in-law of the president.
>
> July 27, 1869 Louis Dent ... Is not in favor among officials at Washington for governor of Mississippi.
>
> August 21, 1869 It has been charged by the opponents of the newly elected United States Senator in Mississippi, that General Ames secured his election to the Senate by the exercise of his military power. Those who know him best say there is not a particle of truth in this statement... He opposed the schemes of Lewis Dent from the first, and at a time when the Republicans were inclined to confide in him, believing that he represented the policy of President Grant. General Ames saved the party by promptly removing from office those who had been prominent in bringing Dent forward as a candidate. The party in Mississippi was young, inexperienced, and

undisciplined, as was shown in the desire of some of its prominent representatives to make a political hero of Dent, who was without character, ability, or real influence.

September 10, 1869 The Republican State Convention in Mississippi met in Jackson on the 8th ... Lewis Dent was unanimously nominated for Governor.

October 7, 1869 Judge Louis Dent, formerly of Stockton, where he was regarded as a man of the very smallest intellectual caliber, announces to his friends that his election to the gubernatorial office in Mississippi is certain. ... He was believed to be in full sympathy with the secession movement up to the end of 1862, ... If Dent is not a king among the carpet-baggers it is only because he lacks the intellectual qualities to make him a leader in anything... The probable election of such a man to so high an office forebodes no good to the immediate future of the State of Mississippi.

(Census records indicate that in 1870, Lewis Dent, his wife, and four children were living in Washington DC.)

June 1871 Judge Lewis Dent was arrested in the city yesterday, on a warrant charging him with misappropriation of money. He obtained bail and left last night.

June 20, 1871 Of Lewis Dent, formerly of Stockton California, the New York World of the late date furnishes the following information, which will be read with interest by his old acquaintances in San Joaquin. ... A few days ago to a series of transactions which took place in which Lewis Dent, who is a claim agent lawyer in Washington, received certain sums of money upon the agreement that he would transact certain business. In one instance he was paid five $1,000 bills; in another he received $500; in another a draft for $250 upon a treasurer of a certain company was cashed for Dent; but, upon presentation of it to the gentleman upon whom it was drawn, he said he neither owed Dent anything, nor did he authorize him to make such a draft. ... A warrant was to have been issued for arrest of Lewis Dent who has been here, stopping at the Fifth Avenue Hotel. It was served upon him, and when he obtained bail, he left for Washington on the night train. This is the same Dent who was pressed, or rather pressed himself, in 1870 for Governor of Mississippi, but who is allowed to remain in private life by a very large majority of his constituency.

September 5, 1872 Lewis Dent was fined $500 and cost in the Police Court this morning, for assaulting Reed, one of the editors of the Washington Capital.

April 11, 1874 The Washington Chronicle of March 29 contains an account of the autopsy of the late Judge Lewis Dent, for which it appears that an extensive cancer, heretofore unsuspected, involving the spleen, pancreas, liver, kidneys, and lungs was discovered, rendering the case one of rare interest to the prominent medical gentleman present.

9

Charles Tyler Botts

When Charles was born on March 6, 1809, in Dumfries, he joined the sixth generation of his family to live in Virginia. While his father, Benjamin, defended Aaron Burr during his trial for treason and conspiracy, Charles aroused equally hostile feelings when he betrayed the public's trust in his position as California state printer.

On December 26, 1811, two-year-old Charles and his three brothers were orphaned when their parents perished in the Richmond Theater fire. The boys' maternal grandparents raised them. Charles graduated from the University of Virginia in 1828 and practiced law with his brother, Alexander.

In October 1829, 20-year-old Charles married 19-year-old Margaret Francis Marshall. The newlyweds lived with his brother, John. Charles and Margaret had five children; two would survive to adulthood. The 1840 census reveals he had four slaves.

Charles left his law practice to experiment with scientific farming. He invented numerous labor-saving devices for small, non-slave-owning farmers, joined the reform-minded Henrico

County Agricultural Society, and founded the "Southern Planter." He championed the use of crop rotation, fertilizers and farm machinery to increase productivity.

Charles left all that behind and sailed to California with his wife and children aboard the *Mathilda* in 1848. He had been appointed the U.S. naval storekeeper at Monterey. One year later he resigned. He returned to the practice of law and began speculating property.

At the Constitutional Convention, Charles wanted California to be admitted as a free state. He felt that "free Negroes" would be exploited by capitalists and he wanted only male citizens of Mexico to be allowed to become citizens of California.

September 12. ...The gentleman from San Francisco (Mr. Gilbert) had left out an exceedingly important word. He (Mr. Botts) proposed to amend the amendment by inserting the word "white" before the words "male citizen of Mexico." He hoped it would be the will of the House that no citizens of the United States should be admitted to the elective franchise but white citizens. All he asked was that citizens of Mexico who had become citizens of the United States should be placed upon the same footing with ourselves; that white citizens alone should be admitted to the right of suffrage. He was sure there would not be any objection on their part to this course.

He also argued against allowing a woman to own property independent of her husband, a law that was on the books when Alta California was part of Mexico.

September 27. The only despotism on earth that I would advocate, is the despotism of the husband. There must be a head and there must be a master in every household; and I believe this plan by which you propose to make the wife independent of the husband, is contrary to the laws and provisions of nature—contrary to all the wisdom which we have derived from experience.

In 1850, he served on the San Francisco Common Council, a predecessor of the San Francisco Board of Supervisors. He opened a law office in San Francisco and purchased 160,000 acres in the Sausalito Cove. He had the land surveyed and streets laid out, hoping to capitalize on the Gold Rush. No one was interested.

From 1856 to 1861, he was the publisher of the *Sacramento Standard* newspaper. From 1857 to 1860, he was a justice in the Sixth Judicial District. From 1861 to 1865, he was the state printer. It was from this trusted position that his controversial political beliefs emerged, as explained in the following newspaper article.

> August 27, 1861. A Secession Document. Botts of Sacramento has issued an address to the people of California, which is out and out secession. He says he defends every act of the South and doesn't care who knows it. A large package of these precious documents, written by the man whose paper died from an overplus of brains, arrived in town last Thursday night, and in less than twenty minutes men were traversing the streets [handing] them out to whoever would take one. It was a free thing. It is a disgrace to the State of California that the office of the State Printer should be prostituted to the publication of such incendiary stuff. We are thankful that Botts's political head will soon be decapitated. Let him return to Dixie and revel in the glory of his traitorous deeds while here.

The following are excerpts from "Address to the People of California," the 15-page pamphlet he printed illegally.

Fellow Citizens –

We have, indeed, fallen upon evil times. The arts of peace are forgotten; from the eastern slope we hear nothing but war; the air resounds with the tramp of armies and the thunders of artillery; our fields are wet with human gore, and vultures batten upon the carcasses of American citizens; the laws are trampled underfoot, and the government is converted into a military despotism. Is it not time then, that we should counsel together concerning our public affairs; that we the people should inquire into the conduct of our public servants, and investigate the causes which have converted us from the happiest, to the most unfortunate, people upon the face of the earth? It is in this spirit I address you.

... I do not believe the reconstruction of this union upon its former basis is either practicable or desirable. A universal government for all mankind is the dream of the enthusiast.... What a utopian he would be who, casting his eye upon the map of Europe, should exclaim: 'oh that all these people were brought under one nationality!'... Where there is no homogeneity, there should be no common government. ...

... If your social and commercial relations with the South increased by peaceable separation, what do you care whether you live under the same or separate governments?

... I am satisfied the time will come when all asperities will be healed, when the people of the Southern Confederacy will again be the best customers of the manufacturers of the Northeastern States, and all the better they had been permitted to increase their wealth by the enactment of laws adapted to their particular interests; and the North will then wonder how she could have been mad enough to offer any opposition to the growth and prosperity of those upon whom she depends for patronage and support.

This war can have no earthly effect except to retard and postpone this happy consummation. I have spoken for myself and myself alone. …I have spoken without consultation with any human being, and I alone am responsible for the sentiments I have uttered. If there is a spark of liberty in your breasts I have said enough to inflame it—if it has all been crushed out, the sooner you are subjected to the yoke of the tyrant, the better.

T. BOTTS,
August 10, 1861

During the Civil War, Charles retreated to Virginia but returned to San Francisco in 1864 where he resumed practicing law until his death on October 4, 1884, at the age of 75.

10

Henry Wager Halleck

Henry Wager Halleck was born on the family farm in Westernville New York, on January 16, 1815. His grandfather fought in the American Revolution and his father in the War of 1812. Henry wanted a military life, not a farming life. His mother's brother agreed to have Henry live with him and to provide the boy with a military education. Eventually, Henry was accepted into the United States Military Academy, also known as West Point.

Henry graduated in 1839 as a second lieutenant in the renown Army Corps of Engineers. Third in his graduating class, one year later, he was appointed an assistant professor of chemistry and engineering at West Point. He was then stationed in New York City where he oversaw the design and construction of the harbor's fortifications, and wrote a report for the United States Senate on seacoast defenses, "Report on the Means of National Defence."

Henri Gratien Bertrand, Napoleon's aide-de-camp, heard about Henry's report and invited him to France to review French military installations. After returning home, First Lieutenant Halleck gave a series of 12 lectures at the Lowell Institute in Boston that were subsequently published in 1846 as "Elements of Military Art and Science," and applied by Union officers in the Civil War.

During the Mexican-American War, Henry was assigned to duty in California. On the seven-month voyage aboard the USS *Lexington*, he served as aide-de-camp to Commodore William Shubrick and spent his free time translating Henri Jomini's "Vie Politique et Militaire de Napoleon," further enhancing his reputation as a military scholar.

Henry arrived at his post in California on August 13, 1847, and was immediately appointed the secretary of the interior by then Military Governor Richard Mason. In addition to being a distinguished member of his corps, Henry was also a trained lawyer and fluent in modern languages.

His first opportunity to engage in combat occurred on November 11, 1847, during Shubrick's capture of the port of Mazatlán. Lieutenant Halleck served as lieutenant governor of the occupied city and was awarded a brevet promotion to captain in 1847 for his "gallant and meritorious service" in California and Mexico.

Henry took it upon himself to maintain cordial relations with the first families in the Californio settlements south of Monterey. He translated the Mexican laws in effect at the time of the conquest, enabling Governor Mason to operate the military government until Congress acted to declare California a territory. He also oversaw the collection of import duties, which provided the military government with sufficient operating funds.

When Brevet Brigadier General Bennet C. Riley replaced Mason as the military governor of California, Henry was appointed the military secretary of state and transferred north to Monterey. It was his plan for a constitutional convention that

The Delegates of 1849

Governor Riley wholeheartedly accepted. In addition to being an elected delegate, he served as the governor's representative at the Constitutional Convention.

Henry would become the principal author of the Constitution. He gave more studious thought to the wording of the document than any other person. His was the omniscient voice at the back of the room—objectively informing and advising, but also inserting his own opinions on select issues during the debates.

At the close of the Constitutional Convention, Henry accepted the nomination for United States senator but was not elected. He remained in the Army four more years, then resigned to give his attention to the practice of law. In San Francisco, he became the senior partner in the firm Halleck, Peachey and Billings which, by the mid-1850s, was the premier land title practice in California. Drawing on his knowledge of Mexican land grants gained in the 1840s while military secretary of state, he became an extremely wealthy man.

In 1855, 40-year-old Henry married 26-year-old Elizabeth Hamilton, granddaughter of Alexander Hamilton and sister of future Union General Schuyler Hamilton.

He was also a noted collector of "Californiana," obtaining thousands of pages of official documents on the Spanish Missions and colonization of California. Fortunately, Henry permitted Hubert Howe Bancroft to copy the documents because the originals were destroyed in the 1906 San Francisco earthquake and fire.

He also built the Montgomery Block, promoted as San Francisco's first fireproof building, served as director of the Almaden Quicksilver (mercury) Company in San Jose, president of the Atlantic and Pacific Railroad, and owner of the 30,000-acres Rancho Nicasio in Marin County. He remained involved in military affairs, and by early 1861 was a major general in the California Militia.

The Civil War cast a long shadow over Henry's life. He was called back to the Army and appointed to the rank of major general. In quick succession, he commanded the Department of Missouri, the Army of the West, and after the Battle of Corinth, the entire Union Forces, with the impressive title of general-in-chief of the United States Army.

In March 1864, Ulysses S. Grant was promoted to general-in-chief, with Halleck as his chief-of-staff.

During the Civil War, Henry's theoretical approach to preparations for battle and defensive fortifications clashed with the practical, more aggressive actions of his fellow officers. He was a master of administration, logistics, and the politics necessary at the top of the military hierarchy, but his lack of leadership skills prevented him from exerting any control over field operations from his post in Washington, D.C.

Despite his learned treatises on the art of warfare, Henry quickly fell out of favor with President Abraham Lincoln and his cabinet. He spent the remainder of the war isolated from power and overshadowed by men with more battlefield experience.

After Grant forced Robert E. Lee's surrender at the Appomattox Court House, Henry was assigned to command the Military Division of the James, headquartered at Richmond Virginia. He was present at Lincoln's death and a pall-bearer at his funeral. In August 1865, he was transferred to the Division of the Pacific in California, primarily in military exile.

In March 1869, Major-General Halleck was assigned to command the military division of the South, headquartered in Louisville Kentucky. He died unexpectedly on January 10, 1872, of "congestion of the brain" and was buried with full military honors. On his deathbed, he requested that all his personal papers be destroyed.

In 1870, an essay by Judge T. W. Freelon, defending Henry's actions during the Civil War, was published in *Representative & Leading Men of the Pacific*. The following are excerpts from that essay.

> General Halleck has been one of the most abused men in the country. As General-in-Chief he was forced to occupy a position misunderstood, even in the army. It was one of responsibility without power. He had no authority to act otherwise than was approved by the President and the Secretary of War. He would simply advise them, and they would then act as they saw best; with the nation holding him responsible for ... orders that were oftentimes in direct conflict with his own judgment.
>
> General Halleck exhibited a commendable spirit of self-sacrifice in remaining in Washington as Grant's chief-of-staff. ...
>
> The General has certainly betrayed none of the professional jealousy supposed to be characteristic of military men, and which has impaired the usefulness of some of our most prominent soldiers. It was he who first discovered and nourished the war-like qualities of Sheridan. It was he who recommended, first, Buell and Grant, and then C. F. Smith for promotion as Major Generals of Volunteers.... He was also an earnest advocate of the claims of Grant, Sherman, Thomas, Meade, and McPherson, for promotion in the Regular Army. During the war, he was in most cordial cooperation with these distinguished men.
>
> It was Halleck who sustained Grant while in difficulties, both after Fort Donelson and after Pittsburg Landing. ... The pressure brought upon General Halleck by the President, Secretary of War, and several of the Western Governors, for the removal of Grant from all command, was almost irresistible. To save him from being absolutely

shelved, General Halleck placed him second in command to himself, it being impossible to continue him at that time of popular prejudice in command of one of the armies.

Again, just before the battle of Nashville, General Grant became impatient at the apparent slowness of Thomas's movements, and directed that he should be relieved; but Halleck's faith in Thomas was so strong that, although entirely unsupported by the Administration in such action, he assumed the responsibility of withholding the order. A glorious victory was the result of the opportunity thus preserved to General Thomas.

In June 1869, under orders from headquarters at Washington, General Halleck relinquished to General Thomas the command of the Department of the Pacific, and assumed that of the Department of the South, with headquarters at Louisville, Kentucky. ...

One Napoleonic quality, which he certainly possessed in a high degree, was the power of judging and choosing men. Always, from the first, he recognized the lofty military merit of such men as McClellan, Sherman, Lee, Thomas, and others, and the qualities of that most successful of all of them—our present President Ulysses S. Grant.

History will do justice to the great services Henry Halleck rendered his country while performing his arduous and delicate duties at Washington during the war. His negative services were, perhaps, even more valuable than his positive. We believe that General Halleck was the right man in the right place at the right time, and did as much as any human being *could* do under those anomalous and fearful circumstances; and posterity, when all is known, will honor him for what he *prevented* as well as for what he *accomplished*.

PART III

Sacramento District

11

John Augustus Sutter

Johann was born the second of seven sons on February 15, 1803, in the Grand Duchy of Baden Germany. His father moved the family to Switzerland where he purchased for himself and his heirs the rights and immunities of Swiss citizenship. Johann would declare allegiance to two more countries in his lifetime. He would also claim that he graduated from the military college at Berne in 1823, entered the French service as an officer of the Swiss Guard and served in the Spanish campaign. There is no proof these statements are true.

In 1824, 21-year-old Johann did marry 21-year-old Anna Dubelt, and by 1832, the couple had four children. As a breadwinner, Johann was more interested in spending money than earning it. His indebtedness brought legal charges and jail time. He dealt with the matter by abandoning his family and escaping to America in 1834, where he changed his name to John.

John traveled through several western States, spending most of his time in Missouri where he made his declaration to become a U.S. citizen. While visiting New Mexico, he heard stories from trappers and hunters recently returned from the far west that convinced him California was where he could fulfill his dream and build his New Helvetia, New Switzerland. In April 1838, without hesitation, John joined Captain Tripp's expedition for the American Fur Company and arrived in California one year later.

In July 1839, he met with Mexican Governor Alvarado in Monterey and expressed his interest in settling on the Sacramento River. He also relinquished his declaration of U.S. citizenship for Mexican citizenship. Alvarado gave him a passport, and permission to settle on any territory with the stipulation that he return to Monterey in one year with proof of having complied with the settlement agreement. His Mexican citizenship would be acknowledged, and he would receive a grant for the land he had developed.

John chartered a schooner in Yerba Buena to sail up the Sacramento River and claim his land. Ironically, after coming so far and surviving so many dangerous situations, he could not find anyone who had ever seen the Sacramento River or knew its location. Undaunted, it took John eight days to find the mouth of the Sacramento River in Suisun Bay and several weeks to locate the precise area where he wanted to build his empire: approximately 60 miles inland from where his schooner first passed through the Strait of Carquinez before entering the Suisun Bay.

John purchased 300 head of cattle and 60 horses. By August 1840, his colony consisted of 25 men who were helping him erect Sutter's Fort.

Like an oasis in the desert, John graciously welcomed the impoverished immigrants who had barely survived the ordeal of crossing the Sierra Nevada. He freely offered them food, clothing, and shelter, and would send aid to those trapped in the snow-covered mountains.

"The Valley of the Sacramento," wrote Thomas Larkin, "is the unique establishment of Captain Sutter. To protect his settlement from the Indians, he has built a fort 100 yards long and 16 yards wide, surrounded by thick and high adobe walls, [en]closing all the workshops and houses and having large gates which, when closed, gives security against Indians or any ordinary hostile attack. The establishment consists of farmers, blacksmiths, carpenters, shoemakers, settlers, hatters, tanners, coopers, weavers, and gunsmiths, and is of the utmost importance to emigrants on their first arrival in California. Captain Sutter is a man well-informed, a sanguine temperament, and has influence over the greater part of the people of the Sacramento Valley. He lives in expectation of this country coming under the flag of the United States."

In June 1841, John returned to Monterey, where he was declared a Mexican citizen, and received his grant from Governor Alvarado for nearly 50,000 acres. He was also authorized "to represent in the establishment of Nueva Helvetia all the laws of the country, to function as political authority and dispenser of justice, in order to prevent the robberies committed by adventurers from the United States, to stop the invasion of savage Indians and the hunting and trapping by companies from the Columbia."

New Helvetia was further expanded later that year when Captain Ringgold of the U.S. Exploring Expedition, and Alexander Rotcheff, Governor of the Russian settlements, offered to sell him all their land and everything on it, including thousands of livestock, for $30,000.

When General Mariano Vallejo was taken prisoner during the Bear Flag Revolt, he was held at Sutter's Fort from June 14 to August 1, 1846. Although John was an officer under the Mexican Government and bound to it by his allegiance, when the Mexican forces surrendered to the American troops on July 11, 1846, he hoisted the American flag at Fort Sutter, accompanied by an artillery salute.

Sutter's Fort continued to flourish. In 1847, John received 2,000 fruit trees. He had sown over 1,000 acres of wheat, which promised to yield over 40,000 bushels. He owned about 8,000 cattle, over 2,000 horses and mules, over 2,000 sheep, and over 1,000 hogs. By late January 1848, he had established his Fort and completed all the conditions of his land grant. Overland immigrants did all their re-provisioning from his stores, and many chose to lease their land from him.

John had grand plans for the city he envisioned would rise on his property. He would call it Sutterville. He wanted to expand the local infrastructure with an embarcadero on the Sacramento River and housing near the Fort. That meant lumber and lumber meant a sawmill which is precisely what Sutter commissioned carpenter James Wilson Marshall to build near the town of Coloma, 50 miles northeast of the Fort. James was in the hills working on cutting a mill race for the sawmill when he made the remarkable discovery that would obliterate all plans of orderly colonization of California.

On the evening of June 28, 1848, James came to the Fort and showed John the nuggets he had found while digging the mill-race. They looked like gold—and they tested like gold. John returned with James to the mill, where he saw the gold fortune with his own eyes. Blinded by his near-sighted ambition for Sutterville, he urged the men constructing the sawmill to continue working and not speak of the gold to anyone for at least six weeks, until the work was finished and his crops were planted. No one could have kept such news secret for very long.

Within two weeks, John's workers began deserting their jobs and heading for the gold country. No one was willing to work for wages, even for an ounce of gold a day. Construction stopped on the mills and no crops were planted or harvested. Soon news of the gold discovery was printed in San Francisco papers. Everything became a dead loss for John.

The invasion of gold-seekers and opportunists was like a giant swarm of locust. Squatters took over his land and cut down his trees to build their cabins; thieves stole his livestock and sold them. There was no law enforcement to help him protect his property. Nothing like this had ever happened before.

Every delegate at the Constitutional Convention knew the name of John Sutter. However demoralized he may have felt before coming to Monterey, he was given a hero's status by his fellow delegates.

September 4. Messrs. Sutter and Vallejo were appointed a committee to escort the President [Semple] to his seat.

Author Augusta Fink wrote,

A hush fell upon the assemblage when the elongated frontiersman was escorted to his seat of honor by Mariano Vallejo and John Sutter. Don Mariano was handsome in appearance and elegantly dressed in the embroidered clothes of the Californio; the ruddy Sutter was immaculate in an elaborately adorned uniform. They made a most impressive pair as with great dignity, the Spaniard and the Swiss moved forward beside the tall, gaunt Kentuckian. Many who were present remembered when Vallejo and Sutter were sovereigns of rival kingdoms. And few would forget that Vallejo had once been the prisoner of Semple and Sutter [during the Bear Flag Revolt].

September 22. Mr. Hastings. I understand that my friend, Captain Sutter, desires to speak on this question [regarding the eastern boundary]. The House, I have no doubt, will be much pleased to hear him.

Mr. Sutter. I speak English so imperfectly that I shall only make a single remark. Gentlemen who have passed through these deserts and traveled over these mountains, may know something about it; but it is impossible for gentlemen who have come by the way of Cape Horn, to imagine what a great desert it is, and know how impolitic it would be to the State of California to embrace within its limits such a country.

October 8. (Mr. Shannon) ...There you start, and you can find below [Sacramento] another busy, thriving town, containing a large number of inhabitants—how many I do not know; but I believe my friend (Mr. McDougal) can tell what the city of Sutterville contains. ...

October 13. The Convention met pursuant to adjournment. On motion (the President being absent on account of sickness), Mr. Sutter was called to the chair.

On motion of Mr. Gwin, Mr. J. A. Sutter was requested to address Governor Riley on behalf of this Convention, when it shall wait upon him in a body after the adjournment ...
... Captain Sutter stepped forward and, having shaken [General Riley] by the hand, raised one hand to his breast and solemnly said: 'General, I have been appointed by the delegates, elected by the people of California to form a Constitution, to address you on behalf of the whole people of California, ... And, sir, the

convention, as you will perceive from the official records, duly appreciates the great and important services you have rendered to our common country, ... well done, thou good and faithful servant.'

Following the loss of New Helvetia, John moved his family to Hock Farm on the west bank of the Feather River where he listed his occupation on the 1850 federal census as farming. In 1865, a few months after an arson fire destroyed nearly everything, he and his wife left California, and moved to the East Coast, first living in Washington D.C., then Lititz Pennsylvania in 1871. For more than 15 years, he unsuccessfully petitioned Congress for financial restitution of his losses at Fort Sutter.

John died suddenly on June 18, 1880, at the age of 77, while in Washington, D.C. The federal census of that year listed his occupation as "discoverer of gold." At the time of his death, his eldest son John was U.S. consul at Acapulco Mexico and his son Emil, Greek consul at San Francisco.

12

Lansford Warren Hastings

Lansford's birth in Mount Vernon Ohio in 1819 placed him in the sixth generation of his family to be born in America. All that is known of his early life is that he was the fourth of eight children and that he studied law. In 1839, the 20-year-old practicing attorney married 22-year-old Catherine McCord, who would die three years later.

In 1842, a wagon train came through Knox County Ohio on its way to Oregon. The young widower joined the caravan of farmers and their families. When a dispute erupted among the leaders, Lansford found himself wagon master, quite a responsibility for the 23-year-old. He led the group to Oregon where Lansford spent the winter of 1842-43 surveying Oregon City for John McLaughlin of the Hudson Bay Company and served as his agent for the sale of town lots.

Oregon didn't suit Lansford. In the spring of 1843, he led a small party into California, to Sutter's Fort. John and Lansford became good friends. Both agreed that Alta California should shed Mexican rule and become an independent republic. Both recognized that the region offered tremendous opportunity for men with a vision to grab it for their own. They envisioned Americans coming west to settle in Alta California where they would become leaders of an independent state.

Lansford's vision was called Montezuma, located south of Sutter's Fort at the juncture of the Sacramento and San Joaquin rivers. His plans to promote western migration included a travel guide and leading another wagon train.

He spent the winter of 1843 writing his emigrants' guide. In March 1844, he returned to Missouri and began promoting immigration to California through a series of letters to a newspaper. He gave temperance lectures to finance the publication of *The Emigrant's Guide to Oregon and California*. His return to California in 1845 was a significant disappointment.

Instead of thousands of settlers wanting to follow him, only 22 signed up—and only 10 completed the journey, among them future delegate, Robert Semple. Lansford planned to lead the party west along the California Trail that he had written about in his guide, but the group decided against taking the hazardous cut off. It wasn't until the following year that Lansford heard that the ox-drawn wagons of 80 people had gotten trapped in that cut-off and 40 members of the Donner Party had perished.

In desperation, he camped at a spot along the Oregon Trail where he intercepted immigrant parties bound for Oregon and convinced them to go instead to California. His bold effort succeeded. In 1846, more settlers came to California than Oregon.

When he returned to Sutter's Fort, the American invasion was well underway. At the first opportunity, he enlisted in Fremont's Volunteer Battalion and was breveted as captain. In July 1848, 29-year-old Lansford married 18-year-old Charlotte Toler and opened a law office in San Francisco, speculating in town lots on the side.

Lansford was one of the first pioneers to hear about the gold discovery. His interest, however, was not so much in mining the gold as mining the miners. From a base he established in Sacramento in 1849, he traded throughout the northern mining camps. He covered a vast territory and offered liberal credit terms. He became a favorite merchant among the miners. While visiting the gold camps, he spoke out at the indignation meetings that attacked the military rule, making him one of the leading men of the district. He turned down an appointment to become alcalde, but the Constitutional Convention was another matter. The miners voted for him to represent them.

At the time of the Convention, Lansford was renown as a trailblazer and guide for the earliest overland parties to the Pacific Coast. He had considerable knowledge of the geography of the country which enabled him to play a prominent role in devising and fixing the state boundaries. He even prepared a manuscript map that was significant in adjusting the eastern border.

After the excitement of the Constitutional Convention, Lansford returned to merchandising, and an itinerant law practice in the mines. His efforts to redirect Gold Rush commerce away from Sacramento to Sutterville failed miserably, throwing him into bankruptcy. To escape his creditors, he fled to Arizona with his wife and five children. He succeeded in obtaining a federal appointment as a postmaster at Arizona City in New Mexico Territory. He opened a law practice, became a territorial judge, and gained local notoriety by leading the movement for the creation of a separate territory out of the small settlements of Western New

Mexico. Then the Civil War broke out and threw Lansford's life into turmoil.

When the people of Arizona learned that he was an outspoken Southern sympathizer, they removed his judgeship. He had no other recourse but to return with his family to California. When his wife died unexpectedly in August 1861, he placed his 10-year-old daughter in a Catholic convent and set out on a bizarre journey.

He hurried to Richmond Virginia, the Confederate capital, and presented a bold plan to bring the southwestern territories and California into the War on the side of the Confederates. Nothing came of his grandiose scheme, and he again returned to California. But when the War was over, and his confederate plan became public knowledge, he was made to feel most unwelcome.

Hearing of the many disgruntled Confederates who were leaving the United States to establish colonies in Brazil, Lansford visited the region and made arrangements with the Brazilian government to attract potential colonists. In 1867, he wrote *The Emigrant's Guide to Brazil.*

He tried three times to lead the few who responded to his scheme deep into the Amazon jungle. In 1870, 51-year-old Lansford died at St. Thomas in the Virgin Islands, possibly of yellow fever, while conducting a shipload of settlers to his colony at Santarém.

13

Elisha Oscar Crosby

Elisha was born on July 18, 1818, in Groton New York, into a farming family of "moderate circumstances." His parents' families were in the Plymouth Colony in the 1630s. Elisha and his six siblings were required to work on the farm, free to attend school only during the winter. By his mid-teens, he was attending school more regularly and reading law in a local attorney's office. In his memoir, he wrote that when he was 21 years old, his father gave him a small trunk of clothes and $50, and sent him on his way. His uncle, a well-known lawyer and prominent public figure, invited him to Buffalo to continue his legal education.

Four years later, Elisha's career as a successful New York lawyer was assured when he was admitted first to the Courts of Tompkins and Cortland Counties as an attorney and counselor; then, attorney of the Supreme Court of the State of New York; and finally, a solicitor in the Court of Chancery.

In the summer of 1848, vague stories reached New York of gold discoveries in California. The pragmatic Elisha dismissed them as unsubstantiated rumors. On December 1, 1848, President Polk's message was published in the newspapers, along with letters from West Coast Military Governor Richard Mason, former U.S. Consul Thomas Larkin, and U.S. Naval Storekeeper Charles T. Botts. Mason, Larkin, and Botts gave their accounts of the new gold discoveries, and what they had seen on their visits to the gold mines. That was all the proof Elisha needed. The gold fever got him; the only question was how to get to California.

Elisha was a law partner in the office of Abner Benedict, whose client was the shipbuilding firm of Howland & Aspinwall. All three gentlemen were just as curious about the gold discovery. They encouraged Elisha to go to California and report back to them "...whether those fellows out there are humbugging us." Elisha told his employer and his client that he would go to California and spend the winter, then return home the following summer. The truth is, Elisha made California his home for the rest of his life.

He left New York Harbor aboard the steamship *Isthmus* in a cold snowstorm on Christmas Day 1848. Arriving in Chagres, he tramped across the Isthmus to Panama where he boarded the steamer *California* that brought him—and 450 other eager passengers—to San Francisco on February 28, 1849. Crew members began deserting the steamer. Its Captain called on Commodore Jones of the Pacific Squadron for men to come onboard and prevent the ship from drifting out to sea. The passengers were told they were on their own, forced to remove their own baggage, somehow get ashore, and find shelter wherever they could.

Elisha went looking for Dr. Thaddeus Leavenworth, an acquaintance from New York. Thaddeus had come to California as chaplain and surgeon with Stevenson's New York Volunteers. As acting alcalde of San Francisco, he was living in his one-room office in a small building opposite the Plaza. He had built a sleeping bunk in one corner and offered Elisha another corner to lay down his blankets.

Launches were available to transport anyone to Sutter's Fort who was willing to pay from $100-200 for the five-day journey. Elisha had a better idea and made a profit in the deal. He bought a rundown whaleboat and found six men willing to pay him $50 apiece for the privilege of rowing the boat to Sutter's Fort. The eager boatmen reached their destination in about three days. He then chartered the launch for $300 to another party wanting to return to the bay.

Elisha collected his first gold dust at Sutter's Mill when he sold clothes and shoes that did not match his new California lifestyle. At Sutter's Fort, he represented a handful of clients in a couple of lawsuits. His first fee far exceeded what he'd earned in New York for a similar effort. It amounted to $3,000 for three days' work and included a magnificent saddle horse equipped with a complete "California" outfit.

While at Sutter's Fort, Elisha partnered with two men in a plan to purchase land and lay out a town. They paid Sutter for 1,800 acres believed to be strategically situated at the head of navigation on the east bank of the Sacramento River, opposite the junction of the Sacramento and Feather Rivers. In early spring they began their survey of the site, laid out the town they named Vernon and established trading posts that offered goods to weary settlers.

By the fall of 1849, the elevated site was a growing trading point for the Feather River Mines with a population of approximately 700 people. Then the winter rains came, flooding the whole country and surrounding the doomed Vernon with a sea of unnavigable water.

In his memoir, Elisha made some interesting comments about pre-Convention California. The following are excerpts from that memoir.

> There was a good deal of talent in the convention. I don't believe there was ever a deliberative body of men collected with more patriotic sentiments and purposes than prevailed in that convention, or one that went to work with more determined zeal, to accomplish the formation of a good constitution, that should be equally serviceable, conservative, and protective, of the interests of the people. The brief time during which they were engaged in their work and the result of their labors, showed that they applied themselves with energy and determination.
>
> We needed a State organization and government for the protection of our lives and property.
>
> Every man carried his code of laws on his hip and administered it according to his own pleasure. There was no safety of life or property so far as the intervention of law was concerned; there was no police.
>
> It was an unknown system to our people and we were absolutely in a state of chaos, society was entirely unorganized, and the recognition of our status as a state with a state government seemed to be the one essential thing to give us a foundation to start upon.
>
> There was a great deal of work done outside the Convention. ... The time was so short most of the determinations were made by discussions in Committees and interviews. ... A great many of the men most active and influential in the making of the Constitution hardly appeared as debaters on the floor.
>
> If California had not been admitted as she was, I think there would have been a great scene of anarchy and confusion here. It might have led to the organization of an independent republic on this coast, might have drifted into that; that was whispered about and discussed.

With copies of California's first Constitution in their hands, delegates returned home with the task of setting up elections so that the people of California could vote to accept (or not) the document created by the delegates in Monterey.

Elisha returned to the Sacramento District by the end of October. He appointed Colonel A. M. Winn as sub-prefect, to assist in establishing precincts and collecting the votes on the adoption of the Constitution. The election was scheduled for November 13. Employing special couriers, Elisha created 52 voting precincts in the Sacramento District. After the election, he rushed the returns to Monterey where they were to be counted by December 1.

Elisha excelled at the task. The total number of votes across California was 12,872. He delivered 5,929 votes—46%—from the Sacramento District. He also financed the Sacramento District election, paying all expenses from his own pocket, nearly $3,000. The government would eventually reimburse Elisha, 38 years later.

The ballot also contained the names of candidates for the first state legislature, scheduled to meet in San Jose on December 15, 1849. Elisha was elected senator from the Sacramento District. "As Chairman of the Judiciary Committee [at the first Legislature session], it developed upon me to originate and examine almost the entire Code of Laws of the State. I never did work as hard as during that winter of 1849-50," he wrote in his memoir.

On December 31, 1905, a San Francisco newspaper printed an interesting article about an elderly woman who claimed that in 1849, she and her mother played prominent roles in having California voted into statehood and the official documents being safely delivered to San Francisco. The ladies say they are Elisha Crosby's wife and step-daughter. Unverified genealogy records indicate

Elisha was married to "the widow of Seeley" in New York sometime before 1848. The following is a condensed version.

The bill to recognize California as a State was one of five measures packaged as the Compromise of 1850, which also included the controversial Fugitive Slave Act. Realizing the need for a body of California representatives to bring attention to California's statehood bill, a delegation was chosen to go to Washington and make a fight for California's admission to Congress. Among the delegates was General John Bidwell, an early California pioneer, and New York native.

Before his departure, the General was approached by Elisha who asked a personal favor. He wanted to know if the General would meet his wife and step-daughter in New York and arrange for them to accompany the delegates on their return to San Francisco. The General's first order of business when he reached the East Coast was to visit Mrs. Crosby with the news that her husband had arranged for her to join him in California. Having fulfilled this mission, the General and his associates proceeded on to Washington, where they entered into the fight for the California statehood bill. Slave State representatives in Congress expressed bitter opposition which placed the Bill in jeopardy of being pigeon-holed. The Californians were thoroughly discouraged and decided to return to San Francisco to wait for a better opportunity to press their claim.

The General returned to New York and told Mrs. Crosby they would soon be leaving for California. The General told her of his experience on the Senate floor, mentioning that one of the strongest opponents to the Compromise was Senator Seward of New York, the former Governor of that State.

It seems that Mrs. Crosby and Senator Seward had been schoolmates, and had grown up as neighbors in the same town. She suggested inviting Senator Seward to her home as a guest at the farewell dinner she had arranged before her departure. The plan worked!

At the next meeting, Senator Seward did indeed announce on the Senate floor his sympathy for Californians and expressed the hope that his colleagues would admit the State unconditionally, and at once. Days of political struggle ended in a victory for California. On September 9, 1850, President Fillmore affixed his signature to California's statehood charter.

The California party, including Mrs. Crosby and her daughter, departed New York a few days later, on their way to the Isthmus. In response to the General's suggestion to Mrs. Crosby and her daughter to wear heavier clothing in anticipation of the predictable rainy weather, Mrs. Crosby had purchased two umbrellas, little imagining the importance that was to be later attached to one of them.

Immediately after their departure, as the story goes, the General turned over to Mrs. Crosby for safekeeping, the various official documents relating to California's statehood. She, in turn, gave the responsibility to her 20-year-old daughter, Mary Helen who never let the papers out of her sight until they were finally placed in the hands of the Federal officials in San Francisco a month later.

During the seven days and nights crossing the Isthmus through heavy tropical rains in an open boat along the Chagres River, Mary Helen hid the documents in the folds of her closed umbrella while she was exposed to the elements. She kept them there during the monotonous ride on mule back to Panama City where they boarded the steamer *Oregon*, bound for San Francisco.

Elisha left the Senate in 1852 and returned to private practice in San Francisco, specializing in defending Spanish-speaking Californios whose land grant titles were being challenged. He argued over 100 such cases before the United States Land Claims Commission during his 1852-1856 tenure. He would write that the United States Supreme Court "perpetrated the grossest outrages upon equity and common honesty" in its California land decisions in violation of the 1848 Treaty of Guadalupe Hidalgo which had guaranteed Californios the same rights as other California citizens.

Elisha's younger brother Samuel also came to California, in 1852; but died on March 28, 1859, in a revenge gun fight. Samuel and his wife were living in Mayfield where Elisha owned 250 acres. Paul Shore, a squatter, was shot during an argument on Henry Seale's nearby ranch when Henry's brother, Thomas, ordered Shore off the property. The report was afterward circulated that Elisha's brother Samuel, Henry's neighbor, had witnessed the shooting and allegedly did nothing to stop it. Thomas was placed on trial, and Samuel was summoned as a witness. Samuel was on his way to the courthouse when someone called his name. He turned around and was mortally shot by the deceased's brother who had come to town for the trial. Samuel drew his pistol and fired wildly. An innocent bystander was struck in the chest and died a short time later. The coroner's jury found that the shot had been fired by Samuel, who left behind a wife and year old daughter.

In 1859, Elisha traveled to the East Coast to argue some of his land grant cases before the U.S. Supreme Court. He was in Washington during the winter of 1860 where he heard all the Congressional debates pending the secession of the Southern States, saw some of the distinguished rebels withdraw from the Senate and House, and was there when Mr. Lincoln arrived. He remained until after the inauguration. In making up his foreign appointments, President Lincoln tendered Elisha the position of United States Minister Resident at Guatemala. He was confirmed and commissioned on March 15, 1861, and requested to prepare for immediate departure for that country.

In Guatemala, Elisha became friends with Rafael Carrera, the ruler and "president for life." He also served as a presiding judge and umpire on a commission that successfully attempted to avert war between Great Britain and the Honduran government in a territorial dispute. In 1866, Elisha moved to Philadelphia for medical treatment and the following year he sailed to Europe to attend the 1867 Exposition in Paris.

In 1871, Elisha once again returned to San Francisco and resumed his law practice. In 1872, he filed a legal separation from his long-time female companion, Frances Deer, after living together unmarried for "many years."

On June 10, 1874, 56-year-old Elisha married 41-year-old Francis Crandall. Their son Edward was born in February 1875.

By 1877, a severe eye affliction forced him to abandon his 52-year career but it did not interfere with his being elected justice of the peace, a position he held for nine years. In 1889, he was appointed a judge of the Recorders/Police Court for the city of Alameda.

On June 25, 1895, Elisha died from injuries he sustained in a fall at his home. He was 77 years old.

"Probably no amount of scholarly detective work would suffice to determine ... the full content of the personal papers of Elisha O. Crosby, at the time of his death ..."

14

Jacob Renk Snyder

Jacob was born on August 23, 1812, in Philadelphia Pennsylvania. His father was a flour merchant who was forced into bankruptcy during the War of 1812 when a British squadron captured three shiploads of his flour. Wanting a more dependable profession, he started a brickmaking business. Wanting better lives for his six sons, he apprenticed each one to a useful branch of mechanical labor. For Jacob, he chose carpentry.

When Jacob was 22-years-old, he traveled to the Falls of the Ohio River; a year later to St. Louis Missouri; and a year after that to Independence Missouri where he joined a wagon train bound for Oregon. By the time he reached Fort Laramie Wyoming, talk of what lay ahead in California changed his mind. He joined a smaller party heading in that direction. The 11 travelers were without an experienced guide and utterly ignorant of how to navigate the terrain or deal with any hostilities.

A traveling companion wrote,

> I arrived at Sutter's Fort from the Rocky Mountains on September

23, 1845, along with Jacob Snyder. We were in a most destitute condition, our only possessions consisting of our rifles, a small amount of ammunition and the buckskin suits we stood in. We had consumed our last morsel of food that morning. ...

After resting a few days, we made arrangements for an elk hunting expedition on the San Joaquin with Captain Sutter furnishing our outfits for which he was to receive a percentage of the hunt. We were very successful and made several packs of elk hides and tallow, but were attacked by Indians and were obliged to abandon everything after two days of fighting.

Seeking a home where he could use his carpentry skills, Jacob settled in the redwoods near Santa Cruz and started a business of whipsaw lumber and shingle-making. In 1846, he applied to the Mexican Governor Pio Pico for a land grant to build a fort for the protection of immigrants against hostilities from the neighboring natives. The governor refused his request.

Jacob heard that John Fremont was organizing his self-proclaimed conquest of Mexican California. Joining the fight would give him an outlet for what he believed were his inalienable rights. He enlisted in Fremont's California Battalion at Monterey and was commissioned a quartermaster. Ironically, in 1848, after the Mexican-American War, Military Governor Mason appointed him surveyor-general of the Middle Department of California with the responsibility of settling disputed land grants in Sacramento.

Jacob is perhaps best remembered during the Constitutional Convention for calling out William Gwin on his motives for coming to California and getting himself elected a delegate. Gwin had made it known to other delegates that he intended to be elected California's first United States Senator, but no one besides

Jacob fully understood the southerner's intention to vote California into the Union as a slave state.

Jacob was described by a fellow delegate as a bold, outspoken man of large physique, as tall as Gwin, and with a rather imposing presence. He said he understood that Mister Gwin had not only come to the Convention to be elected its president but had also brought with him prepared copies of the Iowa Constitution that he expected to have adopted at his dictation. Jacob was the only delegate who could have exposed Gwin's cunning plan without appearing to insult him. The other delegates just laughed, which quickly diminished any possibility of Gwin disputing his accusation.

After the Constitutional Convention, Jacob shed his rugged persona and joined the banking firm of James King of William in San Francisco. He was also elected state senator. In 1850, the 39-year-old married 27-year-old Suzan Brayton. Their only child, Marie Rebecca, was born four years later. Suzan died in 1871. In 1874, 59-year-old Jacob married 21-year-old Rachel Sears.

In 1853, President Franklin Pierce appointed Jacob as the U.S. assistant treasurer at San Francisco, a position he held for eight years during the presidential terms of Franklin Pierce and James Buchanan. He was also active in the Society of California Pioneers, serving as its president in 1854.

In 1859, Jacob purchased 74 acres in Sonoma Valley, naming his rancho, El Cerrito. Within three years, he had 30 acres of grapevines under cultivation. The 1860 California census listed the value of his real estate at $95,000. Ten years later, his property was valued at $115,000.

In 1862, he retired from public life to spend his days at El Cerrito. In 1868, he was appointed a trustee of the Sonoma School District and later that year, served as a grand jury foreman.

The year he retired, he was elected president of the California Wine Growers Association. Two years later, El Cerrito was recognized as a renowned Sonoma vineyard.

> July 1869. Just received from the celebrated Sonoma vineyard of Major J. R. Snyder, red wine vintage 1864, member of Vinicultural Society, ...

> July 1872. Upon entering this valley, the eye is at once attracted by the very extensive vineyards, which in reality give the appearance of one large vineyard. Near the town of Sonoma are the larger wineries of A. Haraszthy, J. R. Snyder, M. Vallejo, ...

> California Wines. The following paper was read by Maj. J. R. Snyder, before the Grape Growers Association of Napa and Sonoma, at its session of July 13, 1872.

> We have observed an article stating that many of our largest winegrowers and winemakers are in the Atlantic states looking for a market for their wines; and that the principal objection Eastern dealers and consumers set up against our lines is that they are too strong in alcohol. Also, that our wines contain all the way from 15% to 20% of alcohol, and that the cheap and popular French and German lines contain from 8% to 10%. It is stated that the German Rhenish wine used among the real and constant wine drinkers of the Atlantic states contains only 7% of alcohol.

> April 1874 A dinner was given by the Sonoma Vinicultural Club on Tuesday the 7th to Maj. JR Snyder, who soon starts upon a tour of observation to the Atlantic States. ... Major Snyder will visit the wine countries of the Eastern States and will post himself on their modes of cultivation and manufacture, with a view to give the club the benefit of any and all ideas that he may pick up in his travels.

<u>March 1875</u> Maj. JR Snyder and W Craig, a committee appointed by the Vinicultural Club, have reported as follows: The Committee to whom was referred the matter in relation to exhibiting our wines at the Centennial Celebration in Philadelphia in 1876 beg leave to report that we recommended that the winegrowers of Sonoma County be requested to meet with the Sonoma Vinicultural Club ... For the purpose of taking such steps in the matter as may seem advisable.

On April 28, 1878, Jacob died of a heart attack at El Cerrito. He was 66 years old. His remains were entombed in the family vault on the property.

15

Morton Matthew McCarver

Morton was born on January 14, 1807, in Lexington Kentucky. Soon after his birth, his parents joined the United Society of Believers in Christ's Second Appearing, more commonly known as the Shakers. Unfortunately for Morton, his mother's prominence in the Shaker community "killed" him.

In 1821, 14-year-old Morton rebelled against the narrow, cramped, religious atmosphere by running away from home. He wandered for a few years through Texas and Louisiana before realizing that he was better off at home under his parents' roof. When he arrived home, his mother told him that his father had died, then she refused to let him stay. According to Shaker rules, they were now dead to each other on earth. Morton would spend the rest of his life searching for a home to call his own.

In May 1830, in Peoria Illinois, 23-year-old Morton married 21-year-old Mary Ann Jennings. Two years later, when the Black Hawk War broke out, he enlisted as a foot soldier in the Illinois militia. The following year he moved with his in-laws across the Mississippi to what would become the Iowa territory and founded his first town, Burlington. During the 1830s, he profited from the sale of town lots and surrounding farmland. He also attempted to build another town.

By the early 1840s, hard times had enveloped the Iowa Territory. Morton, with thousands of dollars in worthless notes and $10,000 in debt, left it all behind. He and his family joined 1,000 pioneering families in "The Great Migration" from Independence Missouri to Willamette Valley Oregon.

Once in Oregon, he made a land claim and, with Peter Burnett, founded his third town in 1843. Linnton is now a suburb of Portland. The land was ideally suited to farming. Morton grew award-winning apples, pears, plums, and currants, opened a merchant house, and was elected presiding officer to the new government's legislative committee.

In November 1846, Morton's wife died, leaving him with two children. In January 1848, 41-year-old Morton married 23-year-old Julie Ann McCoy. They would have three children.

In August 1848, when news of the California gold discovery reached Oregon, Morton joined one of the first Oregon parties headed to the Sierra gold fields. After mining a claim on the Feather River for a couple of months, he felt there were better opportunities at Sutter's Fort.

In December 1848, when Sacramento was being laid out two miles south of the Fort, Morton purchased lots, opened a merchandising exchange, and ran his schooner to and from San Francisco, carrying people and goods. When the first "49ers" arrived, he was established as one of Sacramento's leading men. Politically, he allied himself with the older, anti-military rule of Sacramento Valley settlers.

In early 1849, he addressed a public meeting called by Sacramento's merchants who opposed alcalde rule. They intended to elect their own district legislature.

After Governor Riley's Proclamation calling for a constitutional convention, Morton was elected a delegate. He brought to Monterey 25 years of pioneering experience, bitterness at the financial forces that had once ruined him, and a deep hatred of slavery.

Although he was in California and a delegate from Sacramento, Morton would often refer to his Oregon constituents when speaking on the floor, and what they would say as if they were part of California. He was continually making blunders and getting things mixed up.

After the Constitutional Convention, Morton spent the next 25 years continuously moving between California, Oregon, and Washington.

His farming skills were evidently quite good as judges remarked that the pears he entered in the Agricultural Fair in San Francisco in the fall of 1853 were the finest they had ever seen and "excelled in beauty." The following February he received a silver medal, "as a premium for the best display of fruit" by the California Agricultural Society.

In the mid-1850s, floods and fires wiped out his holdings in Sacramento real estate; he left California and returned to Oregon. Unfortunately, his long absence labeled him an outsider, considered more of a California politician, a man apparently looking out only for himself.

Near Oregon City, he set up a farm, which remained his base of operations, if not home, for much of the next decade. He did some farming and invested in a variety of enterprises, hoping for an opportunity to be elected to a public office. During the Oregon Indian Wars of the 1850s, he enlisted in the territorial militia and served as its commissary general.

In 1857, he followed the mining rush to the Fraser River in British Columbia Canada. In 1862, he moved to the mining camp at Bannock City Idaho where he worked as a merchant. When fire destroyed his mercantile house, he returned to Oregon, settling this time in Portland. But in 1868, news that the Union Pacific Railroad was coming to the State of Washington inspired him to organize just one more urban promotion, this time on the Puget Sound in Washington territory. He first called the new town Commencement City, then changed it to Tacoma.

This was perhaps his most daring scheme ever. Tacoma would serve as the western terminus of the Union Pacific Railroad. He would live there and wait for the train to arrive. For five years, he lived in dank surroundings near Commencement Bay, overseeing the platting of his city, the sale of house lots and the construction of roads and accommodations.

The Union Pacific did arrive in 1873 and Tacoma was selected as its Western headquarters. But, the railroad's terminal and yards were constructed quite a distance from Morton's property, shifting the growth of the city he built in an entirely different direction.

While on a trip to the newly discovered coalfields, south of Tacoma, Morton caught a cold that only worsened. He died two weeks later, on April 17, 1875, at the age of 68.

16

John McDougal

John was born on April 19, 1817, in Chillicothe Ohio, the fifth of six children to a Scottish immigrant who served as an Ohio state representative from 1813–1815. John was seven years old when his father died. Brother Charles became a brigadier general in the U.S. Army, and brother David became a rear admiral in the U.S. Navy. John also achieved high rank, but a self-induced affliction interfered.

In 1841, 24-year-old John married 18-year-old Jane Palmer. In 1846, he joined the First Indiana Volunteer Infantry Regiment as a lieutenant and served in the Mexican-American War. He later re-enlisted in the Fifth Indiana Volunteer Infantry Regiment.

In 1848, John brought his wife and daughter to California, arriving on the SS *California*. He worked first as a miner and then a merchant in his brother's business, George McDougal & Company, during the Gold Rush.

It's likely John was already a heavy drinker when he arrived in California. Fellow delegates later wrote that his drinking greatly hindered his usefulness at the Convention. He voted against a ban on dueling.

Following the Constitutional Convention, elections were held to create a state government. When asked if he wanted to be nominated for lieutenant governor, John replied, "I reckon I'll take that. I don't believe anyone else will have it."

In that same election on December 20, 1849, Peter Burnett was elected governor and John lieutenant-governor. Peter resigned one year later because of widespread discontent with his administration. As the next in line, John was promoted to governor. He held the office for two years. His recurring drinking, gambling with legislative members, and frequent quarrels over minor bureaucratic matters contributed to his not being re-elected.

Four days after leaving the state's highest political office, he was involved in a pistol duel with A. C. Russell, editor of *The San Francisco Picayune*. He shot Russell's hand. After trying to force another duel with someone else over an insult, John was arrested by the San Francisco Police.

The 1860 census lists his occupation as farmer. It's been said that alcoholism and depression drove him to attempt suicide on several occasions. John died in San Francisco on March 30, 1866, at the age of 48, as reported in the following newspaper article:

> John McDougal, ex-governor, who has been partially insane for a year or two, and imagining himself afflicted with an incurable disease, met Samuel Platt on the street this afternoon and although apparently in robust health, commenced telling him of his illness and his liability to sudden death. He accompanied Platt to his office, and while conversing on the subject, was suddenly seized with apoplexy [now known as a stroke], from which he died at about 5 o'clock.

17

Winfield Scott Sherwood

Winfield was born on September 7, 1814, in Fort Edward New York. He was the middle child of a large family whose ancestors had been living in the area for nearly 100 years. His elder brother John was a prolific inventor.

In 1837, Winfield received his BA from the American Literary, Scientific, and Military University in Northfield Vermont. It was the first private military college in the United States. Following graduation, he returned to New York where he pursued a career in law.

In 1841, 27-year-old Winfield married 23-year-old Sarah Worthington. They would have two children. He went into partnership as the publisher and editor of the new *Glens Falls Clarion*. In 1846, he was elected a member of the New York State Assembly. It appeared on the surface that Winfield enjoyed a satisfying life.

What caused him to abandon his family and career? In July 1849, he was living in the heart of California's "gold country" on Mormon Island when he was elected a delegate to the Constitutional Convention.

From the pool of delegates with legal backgrounds and/or legislative experience, 32-year-old Winfield's remarks are some of the most mature and comprehensive. He clearly knew what he was talking about.

Sept 3: Mr. Sherwood did not for his part see the object of having several committees. It was most desirable that the Convention should organize at once and proceed to business without delaying from day to day the question as to what members were entitled to seats. On motion of Mr. Sherwood, the reporters present were invited to take seats within the bar.

Sept 8: Mr. Sherwood said that the gentleman from Virginia, (Mr. Botts,) was evidently not acquainted with the history of the new sects in the State of New York, ... There have been sects known there to discard all decency, ... without any regard for the established usages of society. It was for this reason that the clause was put in the Constitution of New York. No such thing as an attempt to limit the Roman Catholics to any fixed rules of worship was intended;

Sept. 12: Mr. Sherwood said, that as there seemed to be considerable doubt as to what belonged to the Constitution and what should be embraced in the schedule; he thought the schedule should be referred to the Select Committee. If another committee was appointed, the Constitution would be garbled and incomplete.

Sept. 13: Mr. Sherwood said that this question was a matter of principle. ... Economy should be studied by wealthy people

The Delegates of 1849

as well as poor. ... What effect would biennial sessions have in preventing the accumulation of laws? ... For public convenience annual sessions would be preferable. We are an anomalous people. ... Towns and cities spring up here in a month. The population is subject to extraordinary changes. It may number five thousand now in a certain district, and a year hence fifteen thousand. We have no pre-existing laws that can form the basis of our legislation. ... [W]ithout any previous territorial organization—we have to assemble together a Legislature to enact laws suitable to the condition of the country.

Sept. 15: ...[T]his minority report opens the question as to the power of Governor Riley. ... For myself, I do not think this question should have been brought up here. There should have been no discussion as to his power in this Convention, ... we are the representatives of the people, assembled under a call from the Civil Governor of the Territory. We came here for a specific object — to form a Constitution, and without knowing whether this Constitution will be adopted by the people or not,

Sept. 25: Mr. Sherwood. I cannot consent to vote for any such instructions. ... You must have a County Court near to the residence of these persons. ...When a murder or robbery is committed, if you wish to punish the criminal, you must have his trial where the witnesses against him will attend; ... you cannot get them to go any great distance to wait upon the court. You must have, as near as possible, justice administered where the crime is committed. ...

Sept. 26: Mr. Sherwood. I am utterly surprised to hear such a sentiment advanced by my colleague. ...Public sentiment throughout the world is gaining ground against punishment by death. Although I do not go that far, yet I am for affording an innocent man the last possible chance of preserving his life. If we, upon our Constitution, place the provision that a man shall not have the chance to go to a higher tribunal, what will be the common opinion of the world? ... If you hang him by the neck till he is dead, and then it shall appear that his appeal was good and sound, my colleague would say that he regretted there was not a chance for a trial before a higher tribunal. ... And yet, within the Constitution—the law which is to govern us for all time, ...you have fixed this unchristian principle; ... I trust we will not prove ourselves, in the opinion of the world, so bloodthirsty as this.

Sept. 28: Mr. Sherwood. I think the Legislature would adopt this without any Constitutional provision. We are descending too much into detail.

Oct. 5: Mr. Sherwood. If we should chance at any time to annex a portion of the territory south of us by consent of the people, I do not see why we should deny ourselves that right with the consent of Congress, to extend our Constitution over them. Being citizens of the western coast, it becomes us, if possible, to extend our power. ... I hope, if I live forty years, to see the whole coast populated, and a vast empire on it, so that our power on the east and west will be the greatest in the world.

Following the Constitutional Convention, Winfield accepted the nomination for governor of the State of California.

The Delegates of 1849

(Endorsement for governorship, November 1849) Winfield S. Sherwood Esq came to California from New York where he somewhat distinguished himself in the Legislature. He is a pleasant, agreeable off-handed speaker—a man of good requirements, great shrewdness and a ready wit. He is quite a young man and very awkward in appearances.

Although not elected governor, he was elected a judge of the Ninth Judicial District at the first legislative session. He held this position for 20 consecutive years, up to his death.

In May 1859, Winfield was actively involved in promoting the first San Francisco and San Jose Railroad. The proposed route would reduce an eight-hour trip by stagecoach and steamship to three-and-a-half hours.

> W. S. Sherwood of San Francisco ... states that strong efforts were being made to raise by subscription the $50,000 required to perfect the organization under the general law. ... It is proposed to levy a tax of two-fifths of 1% on the property of the County of Santa Clara, to be invested in the stock of the [railroad] company under the general law passed last winter authorizing counties to take stock in railroads. If that wealthy county determines to take stock in the road it will go far towards ensuring the success of the undertaking. If joined in the enterprise by San Mateo, the completion of the railway will be ensured.

This was the third attempt to raise the necessary public funds. Opponents portrayed the plan as "an attempted fraud upon the tax-payers of the counties." The company was forced to dissolve in June 1860. (The following year a San Francisco industrialist and two of his influential friends created a new SF&SJ corporation that financed the construction of the 49-mile route that was completed by 1864. Today, the Union Pacific Railroad and Caltrain operate over Winfield's original route.)

The 1860 California census lists Winfield as living in San Francisco where he reported his occupation as "clerk." The 1870 California census lists him as living in the Alleghany Forest Township in the Sierras where he reported his occupation as "miner" and his birthplace as Vermont, which is where he was educated, not born. A simple newspaper notice announced his death in 1870.

> Downieville, June 25. Judge W. S. Sherwood died at Alleghany this morning. He was an early pioneer and also a member of the Constitutional Convention at Monterey.

The New York censuses of 1850 and 1860 list Winfield's wife and two children as living with her father. In 1870 and 1875, they are living with her sister, brother-in-law and their children. On the 1880 census, both women are listed as widows. Winfield's wife, Sarah, died in 1891 in New York where she had apparently lived her entire life.

Winfield's daughter married and moved to Philadelphia. She died in 1920 and was buried in the Woodlands Cemetery. While her parents lived apart for most of her life, she brought them together in death. In the Woodlands Cemetery, there is a granite headstone inscribed with their names and dates.

18

William Edward Shannon

Ed, as he signed himself in letters to his family, was born in 1822, in Ballina County Mayo, the largest city in Ireland's northernmost rugged county. He was the youngest of Robert and Ann Shannon's five children. The entire family sailed to the United States in 1829 and settled near Bath in Steuben County New York where Shannon relatives from home were already living.

Brother James wasted no time in establishing himself. He was a member of Steuben's first Fireman Company, organized in 1839. In 1841, he was a member of the Steuben Agricultural Society in charge of organizing its parades. He's listed in the 1845 New York State Register as an attorney practicing in Bath and in 1846, a justice of the peace. This is likely where Ed acquired his own legal training because in 1846 he was admitted to the bar in the State of New York as a practicing attorney. But, it wasn't long before he found another pursuit.

In the summer of 1846, U.S. President Polk announced that he was sending a force of volunteers to the Pacific Coast to fight in the Mexican-American War. Colonel Jonathan D. Stevenson was offered the command to raise a regiment from the State of New York, to be known as the 7th Regiment of New York Volunteers. The corps was initially to contain 10 companies of 100 men each, rank and file. Secretary of War William L. Marcy directed Stevenson that the regiment should be composed of unmarried men, of good habits and varied pursuits, and such as would be likely to remain in California or the adjoining territory at the close of the war. In other words, to colonize California.

Steuben County was designated as a location for organizing one company. Ed volunteered at once to raise that company, which he did. Then the men of Company I elected him their captain.

Captain Shannon's company was sent to Governors Island for training on August 1. On September 26, 1846, they set sail for San Francisco on the *Susan Drew*. They were headed around the tip of South America's Cape Horn, a grueling distance of 13,225 miles. During the voyage, Ed wrote a letter to his brother-in-law, Bartley. His poetic phrasing makes his loneliness all that more heartfelt:

> ... I never knew all the pleasure of having friends, until out on this long voyage, and night after night lying upon the deck and thinking of you all at home, and wishing oh how fondly I could again for but an hour grasp your hand and talk to you. ... Well, this simple letter writing of mine tonight has brought things home, by our own fireside, so near to me as though it were, so nigh to me again that it really looks like reality.

The *Susan Drew* arrived in San Francisco on March 19, 1847, after 174 days at sea, including port stops to replenish. A few weeks later, Captain Shannon's men boarded the *Lexington*, bound for Monterey. During the months in Monterey, Ed formed a warm friendship with Walter Colton, chaplain of the U.S. Navy and alcalde of Monterey. That summer, the men of Company I, with Captain Shannon's permission, assisted Reverend Colton in erecting a school in Monterey. Sergeant Evan described the construction.

> During the summer, Walter Colton, the last of the Monterey Alcaldes erected the first school built in California. It was constructed of a peculiar stone, which when first taken from the quarry, was very soft. After being exposed to the sun and air for a time it became very hard. Some of our men, being both Masons and stonecutters, were needed for the work, so the Alcalde had them relieved from duty to do the fine work on his building, and for this they receive extra pay. It was a good job when finished and stands today as a monument to the skill of Stevenson's volunteers. (Ed would return to this building for the 1849 Constitutional Convention.)

In December 1847, Company I was transferred to San Diego where Ed was both commandant and collector of the Port. His engaging personality made him many friends. Six months later, news reached California that the Mexican-American War had ended. On September 25, 1848 Company I was officially discharged. Ed, like so many others, was headed for the gold country. He purchased a wagon and mule team, and chartered a schooner. He hired ten of his former soldiers, outfitted the wagon with supplies and sent the men 550 miles north to Coloma while he sailed 440 miles to Monterey on business.

Ed met with the military governor, Colonel Richard Mason, and requested to be appointed alcalde of Coloma. In Coloma, Alcalde Ed built a shack and opened a general merchandise store, holding court when necessary. It was said he added a jurist's bench to the already diversified establishment where he wholeheartedly dispensed justice, liquor, lodgings, groceries, and miners' tools.

In preparation for the upcoming Independence Day celebration, Ed paid a rigger to climb the tallest pine tree, cut away all the branches and convert it into a flagpole. At dawn on the Fourth of July, he hoisted a giant American flag and offered free drinks, food, and fun—all at his expense.

In response to Governor Riley's Proclamation, the miners held public meetings to prepare for the election of the delegates. They were held in a hotel still under construction, without a roof. Those in attendance sat on the floor beams while a carpenter sawhorse was the chairman's seat and an empty barrel used for the desk. The first man to address the meeting said he was born in a slave state and he did not want slavery introduced in California. He was in favor of pledging any candidates who might be delegates to see that the clause was introduced that would prohibit slavery.

The next man who spoke said he was born in a slave state and that he left it on account of the slavery and was also decidedly opposed to its introduction in California. Mr. Shannon said he was also utterly opposed to the introduction of slavery in California and pledged himself that if he was sent as a delegate he would introduce a free state clause and use his greatest exertion to see that it became part of the Constitution. It was also Shannon who lobbied the other delegates and eventually "secured the declaration and California's Bill of Rights that neither slavery nor involuntary servitude, unless for the punishment of crimes, shall ever be tolerated in this state."

September 8: Mr. Shannon moved the following as the first and second sections of the Bill of Rights.
Section 1. All men are by nature free and independent, and have certain inalienable rights, among which are those of enjoying

and defending life and liberty, acquiring, possessing, and protecting property, and pursuing and obtaining safety and happiness. (Adopted)

Section 2. All political power is inherent in the people. Government is instituted for the protection, security and benefit of the people; and they have the right at all times to alter or reform the same whenever the public good may require it. (Adopted)

September 13: Mr. Shannon said that his constituents, the people of Sacramento, were as willing and as able as any in California to pay taxes. They wanted a good government, no matter what the expense might be, ...

Mr. Shannon did not know what right this Convention had to put restrictions on the people. It was a body elected by their votes to carry into effect their wishes, not to prevent them from exercising their rights as free men. ... Let them send whom they please, either to the House or the Senate. They are best qualified to judge as to the capability of members. ...

I have another reason for opposing the measure. ... Coming, as I do, from the state of New York, one of the free states—knowing that many men of color there are our most respectable citizens; that they are men of wealth, intelligence, and business capacity; men of acknowledged mental abilities; men who have, to some extent at least, considerable influence in their different communities, and who have all the rights and privileges of citizens of that state—I cannot agree to exclude them here from the rights which they possess there. I cannot sustain any measure which will disfranchise them of any of the privileges or immunities which they possess at home.

On December 1, 1849, Ed returned to Sacramento. In May 1850, he wrote a very long letter to Bartley, grieving the deaths of both his brothers and finally unraveling the mystery of why so many of his letters had gone unanswered. Ed was grateful that his father and brother James had reconciled before James's death. There's more:

> If you yet have James's library I wish you would send it out to me by way of the Isthmus, …. I want to get them and keep them as a sacred relic of him we all loved so well. His watch is the only thing I have of his, in which he gave me before starting, still he is ever with me and never shall be parted from me in life. It is all I have of him.
>
> … Rather than by pursuing any one line of business, I can now look back and see where I have missed the most splendid opportunities of acquiring the finest fortune of them all. When I could have had the Captain Sutter's whole business, the control of his whole concerns out of which a dozen fortunes since been made and he, noble-hearted fool as he is, robbed of his surest sources of princely wealth. I might have had when I first camped where this city now stands (in the fall of 1848) and the old captain was my daily visitor, on his own offer because he said I was the "first settler" any amount of where now the city is built, had I only said yes, and which at this day's worth, land alone, one million dollars, …
>
> This great and rapidly growing city, I could have had at an outlay of almost nothing, one share in the Sutter sawmill, … A week since sold for $25,000. … I was then pursuing the plan I had laid out, green as tens of thousands of others who thought they could make their fortunes by large mining parties. I believed I could not honorably desert my party, and in the end found as others have, that such speculations are anything but what we anticipate.
>
> My trading operations ended a little better. I ended them last November as convenient as I could. This in the early part of the gold

discovery was the easiest and surest method of securing a fortune. Traders were comparatively few, prices and profits were very great.

August of last year I was most unexpectedly elected a delegate from the district of Sacramento in a convention of the State of California. I was honored with the largest vote given to any number, and for this and other reasons I could not decline, though it was serious injury to me indeed.

I closed trading at Coloma in December ... And when my collections are all made, will come off handsomely. I was also last summer appointed Judge of first instance but on account of my business, I resigned. I was afterward also, until our new courts were established this spring, appointed District Attorney. These different positions, unsought on my part, have given me a rather prominent and influential place. ...

On October 7, 1850, Ed was elected state senator from Sacramento. The next day, a passenger aboard the *New World* steamship got off when it docked in Sacramento and collapsed on the wharf, dying from cholera. The ensuing epidemic killed 800-1000 people in less than three weeks.

Thousands fled the city in panic, leaving the stricken behind. Ed refused to leave. Instead, he stayed and visited the sick and distressed, doing what he could to relieve their suffering, even providing for their burials.

Early on the morning of November 3, 1850, 28-year-old Ed collapsed, having caught the deadly disease. He died that evening. His grieving friends buried him beneath the oaks that stood just on the outskirts of the city, between it and the old fort. No memorial was placed to mark the spot.

Probate records list the sum total of his estate to be $75: the estimated value of one iron bedstead, one dozen law books, one trunk filled with books, and one picture. Was the trunk of books the one he asked Bartley to send him? And whose image is in the picture? There was no further description. There are also no public images of Ed, but we have a friend's description:

> He was of moderate proportions, a florid, open countenance, with a laughing devil in his eye. He had the spirit of the elves of his own green isle, was ever full of fun and frolic. Many of his associates suffered sorely from his raillery. He was not however malicious, a current of good humor ran through all his acts, showing that a fun loving spirit was the sole mover.

PART IV

San Diego District

19

Miguel de Pedrorena

Miguel was born into a wealthy and prestigious family in Burgos Castille-Leon Spain on January 5, 1806. Those credentials and his intelligence enabled him to complete his formal education at Oxford University in London England.

He sailed into San Diego in 1838 as part owner and supercargo of the South American brig, *Delmira*. He was also the agent for McCall & Company of Lima Peru. In May 1842, 36-year-old Miguel married 16-year-old Maria Antonia Estudillo, the sister of his business partner. They would become the parents of five children.

In 1845, Maria Antonia was granted the 40,000-acre Rancho El Cajon, once part of Mission San Diego. In 1846, she was granted the 48,861-acre San Jacinto Nuevo Rancho in present-day Riverside County.

During the Mexican-American War, Miguel joined the California Battalion and was promoted to captain, serving as the aide to U.S. Navy Commodore Robert Stockton. Following the war, he was the justice of the peace of San Diego for a year, then U.S. customs collector.

Miguel did not appear at the Constitutional Convention until Tuesday of the third week when his fellow delegate, Henry Hill, announced his arrival and moved that he be qualified and authorized to take his seat. He voted regularly and spoke once on October 10th, informing his fellow-delegates that he was in favor of a state government, and believed this was also the will of his constituents.

Despite his prestigious education, vast land grants, and trading business, Miguel was not a wealthy man. For years, his family had been writing to him, urging him to return to Spain and bring his wife and children. His pride prevented him from accepting their offers. Did something happen in Monterey to change his mind?

Soon after returning home from the Constitutional Convention, he made it known that he had decided to return to Spain. While planning for the voyage, 44-year-old Miguel suffered a massive stroke and died on May 31, 1850. His wife, Maria Antonio, would die the following February, her youngest child still an infant. The orphaned children were raised by Maria's mother, doña Maria Victoria Estudillo.

20

Henry James Hill

The known details of Henry's life are not as adventuresome as many other delegates. Reliability defined his life journey.

Henry was born in Culpeper Virginia on February 13, 1816. He was the sixth of nine children, and the fifth generation of his family to be born in Virginia.

He was educated in the mercantile business and employed in a counting house in Baltimore. In December 1837, 21-year-old Henry married 21-year-old Frances Everline. He served as postmaster under two U.S. presidents: Martin Van Buren and William Harrison, and later as a clerk by a third, James Polk.

Henry came to California during the Mexican-American War where he served as a paymaster. He was stationed in San Diego when Military Governor Bennet Riley called for an election of delegates to the Constitutional Convention. Henry was elected as a delegate to represent San Diego.

He was in his seat at Colton Hall on the first day and diligently participated throughout the entire six weeks.

October 6. Mr. Hill. All I ask for the people of San Diego is that they may have a chance of reading this Constitution before they vote upon it. If we adjourn upon the 9th, this Constitution has to be made up and sent to San Francisco. Taking into consideration the length of time that it will require to print and distribute it, I consider the time allowed altogether too short. If there were express horses on the road, it might do; but there are none. I think the shortest time that you can possibly make your Constitution reach San Diego would be about the day of the election. There would not one in twenty have a chance of reading it. If the House orders copies to be written and furnished to the District of San Diego, by the delegates when they leave here, I have no objection. ...

October 8. Mr. Hill. So far as the basis of the plan reported by the Committee goes, I have no objection to it, except in relation to the apportionment which it fixes in the lower districts. It allows the Districts of San Diego and Los Angeles, two Senators, jointly. I object to that. If in order, I propose to amend the report so that the District of San Diego shall elect one Senator, and the District of Los Angeles one Senator. Let the report stand as it now is, so far as it regards the upper districts. The interests of Los Angeles and San Diego are distinct and separate. They have separate seaports. I want this representation divided.

October 10. Mr. Price withdrew his proposition, to allow Mr. Hill to propose the following: The boundary of the State of California shall be as follows: Beginning at the point on the Pacific Ocean, south of San Diego, to be established by the Commission of the United States and Mexico, appointed under the treaty of the 20th February 1848, for running the boundary between the territories of the United States and those of Mexico; and thence along said line, until it reaches the mouth of the Rio Gila; thence along the center of the Rio Colorado, until it strikes the 35th degree of north latitude; thence due north, until it intersects the boundary line between Oregon and California; thence southerly along the coast of the Pacific, including all the islands and bays belonging to California, to the place of beginning. The question [of the boundary] was then taken on Mr. Hill's proposition, and it was adopted, ...

When the Constitutional Convention adjourned, Henry returned to his farm in Virginia, where his wife and three children had been waiting for him. There would be three more children.

In 1861, he returned his commission and all public property under his charge to the U.S. Government to join the Virginia Confederate Forces. He was appointed paymaster with the rank of colonel and served until 1865.

At the close of the Civil War, Henry returned to the privacy of country life, "to some extent broken in spirit and shattered in health." He died on August 11, 1866, in Orkney Springs Virginia at the age of 50.

PART V

San Francisco District

21

Edward Gilbert

Edward was born in 1819 in Cherry Valley, Otsego County New York. In an article memorializing him after his death, it stated that "Most of his relatives are believed to have died before him and little is known of his early days except that he was, in the best sense of the word, *a self-made man.*"

What is known is that he learned the printing/newspaper trade, and in 1839, moved to Albany New York to work for the *Albany Argus*. He started as a compositor, later promoted to an associate editor. He quit the *Argus* when news arrived of the Mexican-American War and the call for volunteers.

Edward joined the New York Volunteers and was appointed lieutenant of Company H. To his great disappointment, his regiment never saw battle. When they arrived in San Francisco in March 1847, he was assigned as deputy collector of the Port of San Francisco.

Six months later, a San Francisco newspaper printed Edward's article, "Statistics of San Francisco." Was this the industrious journalist wanting to familiarize himself with what he hoped would be the continuation of his journalism career?

The amount of detail in the article is enormous, including every conceivable piece of data about San Francisco and its inhabitants. The 459 residents were listed according to race, nativity, age, gender, literacy, occupation and place of business. There is enough information about the physical layout of the city for someone to reconstruct it without ever having seen it in person.

Following his discharge from the New York Volunteers in September 1848, Edward and his partners, businessman Edward C. Kemble and printer George C. Hubbard bought out *The Star and Californian*. They renamed the weekly paper *Alta California*, and Vol. 1, No. 1 was printed on January 4, 1849.

> This press will be independent of all parties, cliques, and persons. The cause which it will assert is the cause of California — the interests which it will endeavor to advance are the interests of California, and the right which it will lend its aid to establish and preserve are the rights of the citizens of California ...
>
> The unenviable position which this sheet at present occupies, of being the only paper printed in California, renders it imperatively necessary, were there no higher considerations, that it should be independent and fair. The publishers are fully sensible that unless such is the course it can accomplish but little in any cause, and nothing in a country so peculiarly situated as this.

From his desk at the *Alta*, Edward was at the epicenter of San Francisco's political turbulence for several months before he was elected as a delegate to represent the citizens of San Francisco at the upcoming Constitutional Convention. From the first day, Edward, the youngest delegate, expressed his thoughts and opinions on numerous matters. Many other delegates were in agreement with what he had to say.

September 19. Are we to attempt here to turn back the tide of freedom which has rolled across from continent to continent? Are we to say that a free negro or Indian, or any other freeman, shall not enter the boundaries of California? I trust not, sir. Under the former action of this House; under the feelings and principles that have been maintained upon this floor, it would be unjust. Neither slavery nor involuntary servitude, unless for the punishment of crime, shall ever be tolerated in this State; and yet you say a free negro shall not enter its boundaries. Is it because he is a criminal? No, sir — it is simply because he is black. Well might it be said in the words of the revolutionary writer: "You would be free, yet you know not how to be just." It has been asserted that our constituents expect us to put such a provision in the Constitution. Gentlemen who know this may be right in advocating it; but I do not believe my constituency expect it, nor do I believe it is the desire of a majority of the people of California. I therefore oppose it.

But, sir, we must go a little further than our constituents in settling this question. The people will consider our acts in this Convention, and if they ratify them, those acts will go before the Congress of the United States; and not only there, but before the great public of the United States, and before all the nations of the world. Does any gentleman here believe, sir, that there is a man who has ever contended upon the floor of Congress for free soil and free speech, and for the universal liberty of mankind, who will sanction a Constitution that bears upon its face this darkest stigma? Even here in California, I do not believe such a provision would be sanctioned or approved. If it should be approved here, it will never be approved there. I tell you, gentlemen you jeopard the interests of California far more by inserting this in your Constitution than by any other measure you can introduce. But I have another objection to it. I find on glancing at the Constitution of the United States, under article fourth, section 2d, that —

"The citizens of each State shall be entitled to all the privileges and immunities of citizens in the several States."

It was a journalist's dream, attending a historic event as both a witness and a participant. In February 1850, Edward traveled to Washington with fellow newly-elected representative George Wright, and Senators John Fremont and William Gwin. On March 1, Edward and George made their formal demands for the admission of California into the Union to the House of Representatives. Nearby, Senators Fremont and Gwin made their formal demands to the Senate.

The Congressional debates kept the California delegates on the East Coast for some time. On June 4, the Citizens and Printers of Albany, where Edward's career had begun, honored their friend and associate with a public dinner in Congress Hall. The *Albany Argus* devoted eight solid columns to a report of the festivities' proceedings. In his humble remarks, Edward was deeply touched by the overwhelming recognition of himself and his accomplishments.

The California Delegate Committee was still in Washington when President Zachery Taylor died on July 9, following a brief illness. Vice-President Millard Fillmore assumed the presidency, throwing the government into chaos. Edward was in the right

The Delegates of 1849

place at the right time, serving as his San Francisco newspaper's Washington correspondent.

Returning to California and his desk at the *Alta*, Edward took his role as a representative of the people quite seriously. In fact, it was his unswerving honor and his scorn for corruption that led to his tragic death.

He wrote an article about General James W. Denver's expedition to aid immigrants reported to be in destitute circumstances on the plains between the Humboldt River and the Carson Valley. The article charged General Denver with negligence and gross mismanagement in the distribution of provisions meant for the immigrants. Edward wrote that some of the supplies were sold to Denver's subordinates who pocketed the money.

Denver denied the charges while Edward escalated his accusations. Their bitter feud played out in the public press. When the general printed a card that challenged the editor's personal character, Edward's unswerving convictions pushed back. He challenged Denver to a duel.

The terms of the duel, scheduled for 5 a.m. on Monday, August 2, 1852, called for Wesson rifles at 40 paces. In the first round, Denver fired into the air, while Edward aimed at him and missed. Denver—and everyone else present—tried to persuade Edward to call off the second round; he refused. Denver's next shot struck its mark, killing Edward.

By newspaper accounts of the time, the entire city of San Francisco and Northern California mourned the loss of so worthy a man as 33-year-old Edward Gilbert. In 1995, he was inducted into the California Newspaper Hall of Fame of the California Press Foundation.

22

Elias Joseph Hobson

Joseph was born on November 8, 1809, in Baltimore Maryland, the fourth of six children. His father was born in England, and his mother's family had been living in Nantucket Massachusetts since the early 1700s. He was 10 years old when his mother died. The older Hobson brothers left Maryland and became successful merchants in Valparaiso Chile. Is it possible oldest brother George took Joseph to sea with him and taught him the business?

L. Hobson & Company of Valparaiso Chile was a family-owned business known to have a capital of $1,000,000 and a net annual income of between $200,000-250,000. Brother George had been living in Valparaiso since the early 1830s. Married, with several children, he was also the U.S. consul. Brother William had been enjoying a lavish lifestyle in Valparaiso for more than a decade. Likewise, young Joseph became a Valparaiso businessman.

Valparaiso was the first foreign port to learn about the California gold discovery because of its regular sailings to and from Yerba Buena, Monterey, and San Diego. The Hobson-owned bark *JRS* brought the first gold shipment to Valparaiso. When the Gold

Rush began, William was the first person from Chile to establish a commission house in San Francisco.

> WANTED. 5000 pounds of gold dust for which the highest market price in coined gold or silver will be paid by Cross Hobson & Company. February 27, 1849.

Joseph arrived in San Francisco in January 1848 aboard the brig *Lady Adams* and entered into a co-partnership with the firm of Cross, Hobson & Company as a resident partner. The mercantile store must have been quite large and profitable because several businesses in the area used it as a landmark in describing their own locations. During the Convention, a comment was made that "…Mr. Hobson, has at times on deposit in his commercial establishment in San Francisco, upwards of one hundred thousand dollars in gold dust, …"

Joseph served his constituency well at the Constitutional Convention. On September 4, he submitted an amendment regarding the election of officers, and it was adopted. On September 11, he was appointed to the ways and means committee. He was in attendance throughout the entire six weeks and always voted. Three of the nine merchant delegates ran for political office; he was not one of them.

In December 1849 Cross Hobson & Company entered into the insurance business with the following newspaper notice:

> The undersigned have made arrangements to insure gold dust and coin from the Pacific Coast to the United States and England, to the extent of $100,000 per each steamer. … It will be observed that the insurance covers all risks, until arrival at the mint in the United States or Bank of England.

In 1850, Joseph returned to the East Coast and in December, the 41-year-old married 19-year-old Elizabeth Kimball in Long Island. Elizabeth is the author of "Mrs. Hobson's Diary."

In April, 1851, Cross, Hobson & Company brought an action of trespass on a case in the Circuit Court of the United States for the Southern District of New York against Edward H. Harrison to recover sundry sums of money paid, under the above protest, for duties upon goods imported into San Francisco during the period between the February 3, 1848, and November 12, 1849. The jury found in favor of the defendant. Until that time, California was considered a conquered territory within which the United States was exercising belligerent rights. No doubt a considerable amount of money was involved.

Joseph and Elizabeth lived at 119 East 24th Street in Manhattan New York. An apartment at that address listed in 2019 for $3,024,000. Joseph died at home on October 2, 1881, at the age of 72. On the previous year's census, he listed his occupation as merchant.

23

Francis James Lippitt

Francis was born on July 19, 1812, in Providence Rhode Island where his ancestors had first settled in 1636. He was three years old when his mother died of tuberculosis. He lost his father when the elder Lippett moved to Fayetteville North Carolina to establish a mercantile house, leaving young Francis in the care of a maiden aunt and grandparents.

From the details in his memoir, the boy was well cared for and given a good education. His uncle was a soldier who took him along when he went on parade. When West Point cadets encamped nearby for two days, nine-year-old Francis visited them frequently, announcing he wanted to go to West Point and pursue a military career.

Instead, he was sent to college where he soon had to support himself after his father's prosperous merchant business was ruined. During the long winter breaks, Francis earned extra money teaching at various country schools and boarding in students' homes.

With college graduation behind him, Francis's dream of a military career resurfaced when he heard that the *SS Constellation* was preparing to sail on a three-year cruise up the Mediterranean. The frigate was heavily armed and carried a crew of over 600 sailors. He applied to the Secretary of the Navy for the appointment of schoolmaster and was accepted. His duty was to teach the midshipmen the mathematics of navigation.

It never occurred to Francis that the crew had no interest in book-learning.

While docked at Lisbon Portugal, Francis heard of a war going on in France between Dom Pedro and his brother Miguel. With no students to teach, Francis decided to get his discharge at the next port, travel to Paris, and obtain a commission in Dom Pedro's army.

He would accomplish this through the influence of General Lafayette, a French aristocrat and military officer who commanded American troops in the American Revolutionary War and knew the Lippitt family. Francis was confident that the little money he had would be enough to get him to Paris while his fluency in Spanish and French would serve him well.

Port after port, the ship's captain repeatedly refused Francis's request to be discharged, then relented as the ship was leaving the Spanish island of Minorca. Once on the mainland, he paid for lodging in a hotel, hoping to find passage on a ship to Marseille. Unfortunately, it was cholera season in Paris, and the ports were closed. Four weeks later, with his funds and patience nearly depleted, he devised an uncertain plan.

He traveled to Barcelona in a diligence coach along a road frequented by heavily-armed brigands. At one point, Francis nearly shot an approaching passenger pretending to be a brigand. "Just as I was about to pull the trigger he burst into a laugh, lowered his carbine, and sprang up and took his seat by the conductor.

When the diligence coach was within 200 yards of the French border, Francis and his trunk were thrown off. Another coach took the nearly penniless and hungry traveler to Marseille where he sold an overcoat and suit of clothes worth $80 for six francs. He calculated that he could walk the 410 miles to Paris—at the rate of 30 miles a day—in 20 days. He had his trunk forwarded to Paris and started walking.

He eventually made it to Paris, having stopped in Lyons where he approached a friend of his uncle's and borrowed money. In Paris, he borrowed ten francs on his pistol and a few days later pawned his flute. He took lodging at the hotel Voltaire where the proprietress was desperate for boarders as she had already lost several to the cholera epidemic. At that time, the death rate in Paris was reported to be about 1,200 people on average, every day.

General Lafayette did meet with Francis and gave him a letter to the ambassador. In calling on the ambassador, Francis was told the French government had recognized Dom Miguel as king of Portugal but had postponed the recognition of his wife. Until that was done, no commission in a force hostile to Dom Miguel, such as the one Francis wanted to join, could be issued. The question was quickly settled by the total destruction of Dom Miguel's fleet and his retreat, which ended the war.

Francis attempted to make a life for himself in Paris by offering English lessons and translating French daily journals for certain London newspapers and a new political work for the New Monthly Magazine. Alexis de Tocqueville needed "an educated and intelligent American" to assist him in preparing *Democracy in America*. Francis worked with him for several months on the book that would become a classic.

When France refused to make its first payment to the United

States under the Treaty of 1831, as indemnity for American losses by illegal seizures before 1800, President Andrew Jackson sent a message to Congress to appropriate $10,000,000 for "the war with France."

With the opportunity of another war beckoning on the horizon, Francis quickly left for home, hoping to obtain a commission in the Army. On his arrival in New York several weeks later, he learned that there would be no war. Francis put aside his dream of fighting in a battle and took up the study of law. He was 20 years old.

Under the strict requirements of the profession, it would take Francis six years before he could even begin to make himself known as a lawyer. He would need social or political influence to bring him clients as well as financial support until he had paying clients. Francis was penniless, and without any social or political contacts to help him. He studied for seven years and led a solitary life, with one exception.

On his return from France, he enlisted in the Third Regiment of the First Division of the New York State Artillery. In 11 years, he never missed a drill or a parade and was regularly promoted through all the ranks, from private to lieutenant colonel.

By 1838, 26-year-old Francis was a full-fledged lawyer and began practicing law. Five years later, his business had not grown to his satisfaction.

Then came the Mexican-American War. Colonel Thomas, U.S. Army, commandant of cadets at West Point, raised a regiment for the War, known as the "Crack Regiment," of which Francis was a member. When they were mustered into the state service, Francis received a commission.

Every day, the regiment expected orders for being mustered

into service. Word reached them that from the last accounts the war was over, that should hostilities be resumed, no volunteer regiments would be taken from the North. When Francis heard of the New York Volunteers, he immediately joined them and was made the captain of Company F. They sailed for California aboard the *Susan Drew*. Expecting to practice law in California after the war, he took along his small collection of law books.

The *Susan Drew* arrived in San Francisco on March 6, 1847, after a voyage of five months and ten days. A few weeks later, Company F was ordered down the coast to Santa Barbara, where they arrived in heavy seas and had to anchor about a mile offshore.

As the senior captain, Francis was to come off in the last boat with half a dozen men and a lot of rifles, camp kettles, etc. A huge wave capsized the boat. The gunwale came down on his right leg and broke it, incapacitating him for six weeks. When the company was moved into quarters in the heart of the town, Francis assumed independent command of the military district and the Santa Barbara post. How proud he must have felt.

In October 1848, the New York Volunteers were mustered out of service. Francis returned to San Francisco and set up a law office. Business poured in, principally the examination of titles. Every day, many thousands of dollars were spent in purchasing lots and in selling them at an advance often of five times the purchase price. He also bought lots and made quite a lot of money.

Francis and future fellow delegates William Steuart, Myron Norton, and Edward Gilbert, were organizing a provisional government in San Francisco when Governor Riley issued his Proclamation for a constitutional convention.

September 26. Mr. Lippitt. I am decidedly opposed to the amendment for two reasons. The first I have already stated—that all cases under $200 are not petty cases. There are many cases under that sum which involve the most important principles, and require the highest legal wisdom of the country to settle. The second reason is, that it will work oppressively upon the poor if this amendment is adopted. They will bring the great mass of suits in cases under $200; it is the poor who will be the litigants. Then, sir, if this amendment is adopted, you allow the rich man, in all his suits, to go before the highest tribunal; to avail himself of the highest legal wisdom of the land. At the same time, you tell the poor man he shall have the benefit of only one Court of Appeals; that he shall not have the benefit of any higher tribunal than the District Court.

October 4. Mr. Lippitt. That is just the difference between the Constitution, or fundamental law of the land, and an ordinary law of the Legislature. Let the will of a majority of the people always make and unmake laws; they are changing from year to year; but do not let these changes – these transient changes, which are brought about by politicians for party purposes, party majorities in favor of a particular measure—affect your fundamental law. It would greatly militate against the permanent prosperity of the people. The laws of the State can be repealed at any time if they work badly; but if an alteration made in your Constitution is found to work badly, it will take years to correct it. Whether it be democratic, or republican, or otherwise, I would not leave it to the mere transient majority of the people; I would not leave the future interests of the whole people dependent upon that majority.

After the Constitutional Convention, Francis resumed his law practice in San Francisco. Twice, he had to abandon his office when the wooden buildings caught fire. Determined not to be burned out again, he rented an office in the first fireproof building in San Francisco, built by fellow-delegate Henry Halleck. The monthly rent was $125 instead of the usual $50.

It was a two-story brick building, and his office was on the second floor. The iron roof was surrounded by a parapet of brick, and there was nothing in the interior but stone and iron—except the floors and stairs. The front door was iron, all the windows had iron shutters and finally, in the yard was a small fire engine kept ready for use. What could possibly go wrong?

Francis had acquired an extensive law library, valued at $10,000. As a safety precaution, books on the shelves were kept in wooden boxes with handles.

On the afternoon of Saturday, May 5, 1851, Frank Baker stepped out for a few moments from his paperhanger's shop where he had left a pot of varnish boiling. He returned to discover that the container had boiled over and set the shop on fire. A strong wind spread the fire to where Francis's former law partner, Hall McAllister, had his office, on the other side of town from Francis.

Believing his office was safe from the fire, he hurried to help McAllister. Without warning, the strong winds changed direction—towards Francis's office. He forced his way through the crowds and when he got to his building, he saw that one of his window shutters was open. He was able to rush inside and close it.

When he came out, a heavy beam was rammed against the iron door to prevent anyone else from going inside. It was soon evident that the building was not fireproof. The heat from the nearby burning buildings had warped the iron plates on the roof. They began falling through the crevices onto the flammable wooden floors. Everything inside the building was consumed by the fire, including Francis's cherished law library, office furniture, account books, and clients papers. The greatest loss was his irreplaceable professional briefs.

In 1852, 40-year-old Francis retired from practicing law and married Elizabeth Clarkson from Durham England. The following year they traveled to Providence Rhode Island where their son Frank was born in January 1854. The family went abroad on the *SS Arctic*, a paddle steamer known for its speed. (On its return to New York, it collided in the fog with another transatlantic ship and sank.)

The weather in Brussels was unusually hot, and their precious young son died of heatstroke. While enduring a parent's worst nightmare, Francis received a letter from California informing him that his agent had embezzled him of all his property—and wealth. They left immediately for San Francisco.

At the time, there was no law in California designating embezzlement of trust funds by an agent a criminal offense. Still, Francis had him arrested and made him turn over all the property he had bought and improved. It took Francis two years to recover $10,000.

He was forced to rent an office and resume a law practice, but his prospects were not hopeful. During his two-year absence, many clients had died, some had moved away, and the rest had given their business to other lawyers.

In June 1857, their daughter Caroline was born. Two years later, Francis's wife of seven years died from Panama fever, contracted on the Isthmus on her way to visit family in the East.

Francis left California after the Civil War and returned to Providence Rhode Island. With his fortune gone, it was necessary that he continue working. In 1869, he moved to Cambridge Massachusetts and opened a law office in Boston. Cases immediately came to him, and he soon acquired a reputation at the bar as an equity lawyer.

In 1865, 53-year-old Francis married 40-year-old Elizabeth Webb Dodge, a widow with two young children. On the 1880 federal census, Mr. & Mrs. Lippitt were residing in Washington D.C. with their three children. Francis's occupation is listed as clerk, Department of Justice.

In 1882, his 25-year-old daughter Caroline died of tuberculosis, the same disease that killed his mother. Having lost so many beloved family members, Francis and Elizabeth became interested in spiritualism, the ability to communicate with departed loved ones. In 1888, Francis wrote, *Physical Proofs of Another Life, Given in Letters to the Seybert Commission*, whose intent was to disprove the Commission's tested claim that the medium, Pierre L.O.A. Keeler, was a fraud.

> Of such recognition, I will now give some instances.
> At the seance of December 27, 1886, one of the messages was signed " Francis Leonard Lippitt. This was the name of my infant son who died in Brussels, Belgium, in 1854. It referred to something-known to no mortal but myself and a friend in California.
> The following is a facsimile of a writing received by me at the seance of May 26, 1888. The handwriting in the body of it is strikingly like that of the person whose name is signed to it, and who died in 1859: Elizabeth Lippitt, Francis's wife.
> At the seance of March 19, 1886, a message came to me signed,

"Lucy Ann Lippitt," the name of an aunt who died in Providence, R. I., in 1866, and of whom I am positive Keeler had never heard.

At the seance of March 25, 1886, I received a writing signed by the name of an uncle of mine, an Episcopal clergyman, who died in Virginia in 1867. I have no reason to believe that Keeler had ever heard of him. Since then I have received from him at these seances some forty or more messages, all in the same handwriting, which, however, does not resemble his handwriting on earth.

In view of the great number and variety, and conclusive nature of the facts I have presented in these letters, I claim it to be demonstrated

First. That the manifestations through Pierre L. O. A. Keeler are not produced by trick, but by extramundane agencies; and that your Report is therefore grossly unjust both to him personally, and to the cause of truth.

Secondly. That spirit return is a fact, and that there is, therefore, Another Life.

Yours respectfully, Francis J. Lippitt

In 1902, Francis published *Reminiscences of Francis J. Lippitt,* written for his family, his near relatives, and intimate friends. He died on September 26, 1902, at the age of 90, soon after *Reminiscences* was published.

24

Myron Norton

Myron was born on Sept 23, 1822, in Bennington Vermont. Several Norton men fought in the Revolutionary War. After graduation from Harvard, Myron continued the family tradition and enlisted in the Army to fight in the Mexican-American War under General Winfield Scott. Hearing of a vacancy in Stevenson's New York Volunteers, he left for California in 1848.

After his discharge the following September, Myron opened a law office in San Francisco and joined other law-abiding citizens in attempting to establish a provisional territorial government for the better protection of life and property until the United States extended its protection.

The First California Guard was formed July 27, 1849, under the Military Governor Bennet C. Riley. Myron was appointed as first lieutenant.

At the Constitutional Convention, Myron was appointed the chairman of the 20-member committee to prepare a draft of the Constitution for the consideration of the convention. His Harvard education served him well.

September 6. ...The people sent delegates here to form the organic law of what would soon, he trusted, be a great State of the American Union. The proposition of Mr. Gilbert seemed to him to indicate the most practicable mode of proceeding. The Committee thus appointed could report, in whole or in part, a form to be acted upon ... He was not prepared to say they could form a Constitution better than those of the several States; but the Committee could select from them such provisions as were most applicable to this country, and by combining the wisdom of the whole, make a better Constitution than could be accomplished in any other way. ...

September 13. Mr. Norton did not see that we had any power to appoint such a commission as the gentlemen proposed. What authority had members of this Convention to appoint three persons to form a code of laws for the Legislature? ... We have no laws here. It has been impossible to ascertain what the law is, or to enforce it. ...The Legislature of California will therefore have a great deal of work to do. It is said that in new States, there is great danger of hasty legislation. ...

Mr. Norton thought it a matter of very serious importance that persons holding office should be made accountable for the money placed in their hands. It is no small matter that the Government should be protected against dishonest men. Many public officers hold large amounts of money. The people should know where that money goes. ... The gentleman says that a person holding public funds may be unfortunate in business, and unable to settle his accounts at the proper time. If so, he has no business in the Legislature. ...

September 22. ... California is not a new territory, although she seems to be considered so by many here. Heretofore she was but little known; she was regarded as an isolated part of the earth. No one thought of California; no one thought of emigrating here; no one ever thought, previous to the last two years, that she would ever amount to anything. But within the last twelve months, behold what a change! The eyes of the world are turned towards her. The people from every spot of God's earth are starting here, impatient to make it their future home—some to acquire wealth and carry it away. Sir, she has been considered, as I heard remarked to-day, in the light of a courtesan; she had a disreputable character; no one courted her, no one had any regard for her; but since her rich treasures have been developed on the slopes of the Sierra Nevada, she has become a most beautiful mistress.

The whole world is worshipping at her feet. Is it any portion of California? No, sir, it is the whole of California; and I ask members of this Convention, as the representatives of the people, if they can point to any portion of California on the map and say there is California, and the rest of it we know nothing about. Gentlemen may say that a certain portion of the territory is worthless. Have we any right to make that an objection?

September 27. ... I regret that, during this discussion, gentlemen should have made this a question between the common and the civil law. It is taken for granted that if we adopt this section, or that of my colleague, we are going to adopt the civil or the common law. I insist that the question has nothing to do with it; and that the whole course of argument, whether we are to adopt common or civil law is totally irrelevant to the question under consideration. The question before the committee is, whether or not we shall adopt a certain section is introduced here, providing for the security of property, both real and personal, of the wife....

October 12. Mr. Norton submitted the following resolution, which was unanimously adopted, viz and:

Resolved, That the thanks of this Convention be presented to the Honorable Robert Semple, for the faithful and impartial manner in which he has discharged the arduous and responsible duties of the Chair; and that in retiring therefrom he carries with him the best wishes of this Convention.

After the Constitutional Convention, Myron settled in Los Angeles where a prominent judgeship career awaited him. In 1851, he was elected a judge of the Superior Court, and in 1852, elected to the Common Council, the city's governing body. In 1854, he was a judge of the County Court of Los Angeles, often called to Santa Barbara on essential cases.

In 1855, he was a candidate on the Democratic ticket for a judge of the Supreme Court, the highest court. Three days before the election, Myron was seen on the streets of San Francisco in what appeared to be an intoxicated state. It was enough to destroy his chance of ever winning an election

In 1860, 38-year-old Myron married 30-year-old Pilar Lugo. The couple had two children but the marriage did not last. The 1870 Los Angeles census lists Myron living at one address, and his family at another.

He served out his time as county judge and practiced law for several years afterward, but alcoholism eventually diminished his mental and physical capacities. The 1880 census lists him as being single, and a patient at the Los Angeles County Hospital and Alms House, suffering from rheumatism. He died on April 16, 1886, at the age of 64.

25

Rodman McCamley Price

Rodman was born on May 5, 1816, in Newton New Jersey, the fifth generation of his family to be born in America. He pursued classical studies at Princeton College but left before graduating because of poor health. Is it possible that his mother's death, when he was 16 years old, had something to do with his leaving college?

He studied law, was admitted to the bar, but never practiced, choosing the "commission business" instead. In September 1837, 21-year-old Rodman married 17-year-old Matilda Trenchard.

In 1840, Rodman was a purser in the U.S. Navy, his duty to maintain the ship's financial accounts. With one exception, his ship engaged in routine coastal cruises. Perhaps seeking a more adventuresome cruise, Rodman joined Commodore John Sloat's Pacific Squadron and was stationed in San Francisco, a continent away from his wife and two young children. At the outset of the Mexican-American War in 1846, Sloat named Rodman prefect and alcalde of Monterey.

<u>August 1846</u>. NOTICE. Whereas, the authorities of the United States deeming it of the first importance to maintain order and quiet, and to give security to all persons, and to prevent any riot or disturbance in the town of Monterey and its jurisdiction. An order was published prohibiting the sale or disposition of any ardent spirits. Notwithstanding the order, the sailors and soldiers of the United States, as well as persons of this place, frequently become intoxicated. It is therefore evident that persons are still indirectly disposing of liquors. It is hereby ordered that no one is to sell or dispose of any intoxicating liquors whatever, and all persons that have formerly vended liquor, and all store and shopkeepers and keepers of public hours are prohibited from keeping any liquors or winds of any kind or description in their shops or stores as so doing will be considered a violation of this order and will be looked upon with the greatest severity and punished by forfeiture of their liquors, fine and imprisonment at the discretion of the magistrate, Monterey, August 13, 1846. (Signed) Walter Colton, Rodman M. Price.

While working under Sloat's command, Rodman became his investment agent and partner, searching for choice rancheros to purchase. By late 1848, Rodman returned to New York where he secured an appointment from President James Polk as a purser for the entire Pacific Squadron. With its headquarters moved to his own waterfront property in San Francisco, Rodman became provisioner and payroller for ships and depots from Monterey to Honolulu. The highly-speculative operation made him a real estate tycoon.

At the Constitutional Convention, Rodman frequently expressed his opinion.

September 13. Mr. Price moved to strike out this section. He believed it to be exceedingly impolitic to prohibit the drawing of lotteries in this country. It might be made a source of great revenue to this State, and however the principle was, yet he believed it was better in some cases to legalize immoral acts than to have them done in secret. ... He regarded the propriety of this policy as too palpable to require an elaborate argument.

He wished gentlemen to reflect before they forever prohibited lotteries in California. He was opposed to the system himself, and would be sorry to see it legalized; but he believed it was a necessary evil in California at this time. Three hundred thousand dollars could be raised annually by the State for the privilege of lotteries. This would be a great relief under the embarrassing position that the State will be placed in when the new government goes into operation, owing to the difficulty of organizing a perfect system of taxation. It would be a very essential relief to the people, and would defray the expenses of their Legislature until better means of obtaining the full amount of taxes necessary to defray the expenses of the government are established.

In December 1849, Rodman was relieved of duty as a naval agent and returned to the East Coast.

April 1850. Dreadful Steamboat Disaster. The steamboat Orline St. John was destroyed by fire in the Alabama River on her way from Mobile to Montgomery Alabama in the afternoon of March 5, 1850. ... Many lost their lives by their rashness. ... The total loss is estimated at $600,000, much of which was individual property. Purser Rodman M. Price was on board and lost a safe containing $250,000 of government funds. [Also lost in the fire were all his personal possessions, including receipts and vouchers.]

He returned to New Jersey, reunited with his wife, and fathered three more children. With his business partner, Samuel Ward, he established the New York office of Ward & Price, Bankers and Agents for California. He was elected to the House of Representatives and served from March 4, 1851–March 3, 1853, but was not re-elected.

He ran for Governor of New Jersey the following year and was elected, serving from 1854–1857. During his tenure, a geological survey was authorized, a railroad monopoly question was resolved, the state militia was restructured, and the state's school system was vastly improved. Ineligible for a second term, Rodman retired from politics to his farm in New Jersey. In 1861, he was a delegate to the Peace Conference in Washington, D.C., a coalition organized in the hopes of diffusing the impending Civil War.

Ten years later, a crime was exposed that implicated the former California millionaire in fraud. Were the personal receipts and vouchers he lost in the steamboat fire his entire financial wealth—as well as that of Samuel Forrest?

Samuel Forrest, a fellow naval officer also stationed in California, had acquired a great deal of property. Samuel was called away on another mission and gave Rodman a power of attorney to dispose of his property. Rodman sold it to the government but never sent Samuel any of the proceeds from the sale.

When Samuel died, a bill was entered into judgment in 1874 against Rodman in favor of Samuel's estate for $17,000. Rodman supposedly had no real property that could be attached. The case lay dormant for 18 years. In 1892, an attorney for Samuel's widow heard that Rodman was about to receive $45,000 from the government to reimburse him for private monies he claimed he advanced the United States along the Pacific Coast.

An order was made by the Court of Chancery in August 1892

for a receiver to control any transaction with the money Rodman received from the government. Rodman bypassed the order by securing several large drafts which he endorsed, transferred, and cashed.

It was known that he traveled to his farm in Bergen County New Jersey, and always on a Sunday to avoid being served the court order. However, he was observed making a mid-week trip, and that's when he was handed the subpoena. At his hearing, the chancellor directed the $31,000 still due Rodman to be paid to the receiver on behalf of Samuel's widow. Rodman did not comply and was detained for contempt in the Hackensack jail where he remained for some time until four renowned gentlemen put up his bail.

On May 15, 1894, he was found guilty of contempt with the condition that if he did not pay over to the receiver $31,794 within the next five days, he would be committed to the Bergen County Jail until the amount was paid. The former governor did not go to jail. He died approximately three weeks later in Oakland, New Jersey on June 7, 1894. He was 78 years old.

26

William McKendree Gwin

William was born on October 9, 1805, in Gallatin Tennessee, the sixth of nine children to a prominent Methodist minister whose ancestors emigrated from Wales before 1600.

William studied law and was admitted to the Tennessee bar when he was 21 years old. It was then that he convinced himself he lacked his father's confidence as an orator. He studied medicine and received his Medicinae Doctor degree in 1828 from Transylvania University in Lexington Kentucky.

In December, 23-year-old William married 18-year-old Caroline Sampson and moved to Clinton Mississippi where he began his medical practice and started a family. The couple became the parents of two sons and a daughter.

Caroline and their infant daughter died in 1828. Two years later, William's two young sons also died. Overcome with unimaginable grief, he abandoned his medical practice and never again spoke of losing his family.

President Andrew Jackson, a good friend of his father's, called him to Washington D.C. where he served as the President's confidential secretary for six months, then returned to Mississippi as a U.S. marshal.

William's position as marshal provoked a latent hostile nature as he openly encouraged a feud against a senator who had objected to his appointment: "If we cannot disgrace him by beating him he shall atone for his attacks upon us by his blood." It was William's brother Samuel whose blood was shed. Samuel continued to harass the senator and was challenged to a duel. He was mortally wounded and suffered for months before he died.

In March 1837, 32-year-old William married for a second time to 22-year-old Mary Elizabeth Bell in West Feliciana Louisiana. The couple had four children. During the financial crisis of 1837 and recession of 1838, the value of William's previous land speculation investments collapsed. Banknotes he held were worthless while claims against him as U.S. Marshal were ordered paid in gold.

In 1840, William was elected a U.S. representative from Mississippi and served in Congress until 1843. He moved his family to New Orleans where another president, James Polk, appointed him to another patronage post: commissioner of public works. Six years later, coinciding with the news of the discovery of gold in California, was a new U.S. president who was less favorable to William. He resigned his post in New Orleans and set his sights on California.

The day before his departure, he told Senator Stephen Douglas that the failure of Congress to give California a territorial government would force its inhabitants to create a state government and that he would be declared a candidate for the United States Senate from California … within one year. It was a prophesy that would come true.

The Delegates of 1849

William arrived in San Francisco in June 1849, having taken the quicker route across the Isthmus of Panama. With Military Governor Bennet Riley's Proclamation issued only days earlier, William wasted no time in establishing himself as a candidate of the people. Claiming to represent the anti-military insurgency, he called for an independent citizen group to create a state government.

He took his anti-military/pro-statehood message wherever he could find the crowds, in large towns such as Sacramento and small ones like Stockton. Despite the brief campaign, his name appeared on most tickets in San Francisco's election of delegates, and he was voted in.

In addition to his plan to be the first state senator, William made it known to his fellow delegates on their way from San Francisco to Monterey that he considered himself the obvious choice for president of the Convention. Yet, when the time came for that election, the equally-impressive Jacob Snyder called Gwin's bluff.

He said he understood that Mister Gwin had not only intended to be elected president but had also brought with him prepared copies of the Iowa Constitution which he expected to have adopted according to his dictation. The bold frontiersman was the only delegate who could have publicly exposed William's scheme without appearing to insult him outright and cause any dissension. When the laughter subsided, Jacob nominated a fellow settler, Robert Semple, who easily won the vote.

As one of the older members of the Convention, and the only one with congressional experience, William was also the most talkative. Throughout the convention's 37 working days, his name appears in the transcript 461 times, either as a speaker, referenced by another speaker, or voting. The second most talkative delegate's name is mentioned 451 times, and the third, 286 mentions.

September 17. Mr. Gwin. If I do not prove it, then my argument is worth nothing. I do not intend to consume the time of this house, by going into a discussion of the bank question. The question, sir, has been settled. Public opinion throughout the United States is against the banking system. All I want to show is that there are dangerous provisions in these articles granting privileges to corporations of this character. ...

I was somewhat surprised, Mr. Chairman, that the Chairman of the Committee did not put this construction on my motion, and proceed to defend the position of the majority of the Committee as embodied in the report on the subject of corporations; this is the usual course in all parliamentary bodies with which I am acquainted. ... I had a right to expect that the Chairman would pursue this course, but I waive it, with a single remark in reply to his assertion, that the difference between the majority and minority reports are merely verbal. There never was a greater mistake; they are as widely separated as if the Pacific lay between, as I will proceed to show.

It is with most unaffected reluctance, Mr. Chairman, that I engage in the discussion of this question at all. I did hope that it had been completely settled by the advancing spirit of the age, ... But I am mistaken and am called on most reluctantly to buckle on my armor, worn in many a hard-fought battle on this subject, and which I hoped was laid aside forever, and battle for the rights of the people, against monopoly and the legalized association of wealth to appropriate the labor of the many for the benefit of the few.

It wasn't until the boundary question was introduced that William revealed his deep-seated Southern loyalties. After two years as a state senator, he was still pursuing the idea of making California a slave state.

The Reverend Samuel Willey, also in attendance at the Constitutional Convention as the minister who offered the morning prayer, overheard Gwin in a conversation some years later. Rev. Willey wrote,

> ... I learned it in a very direct way. I had occasion to go from San Francisco to Monterey on the steamship Panama on September 15th, 1851. Senator Gwin was on board, on his way to Washington. Governor McDougal was also on board, on his way to Monterey and other towns south to attend conventions called to express a desire of the people for a division of the state, ostensibly on account of the non-adaptation of laws both to the north and to the south—on equal representation, unjust taxation and so forth.
>
> But there was another reason beneath all that, which soon appeared in a conversation between the governor and the senator. Said the senator, speaking of the proposed division, [of California into a free state and a slave state] "The country is right for it, North and South. The initiatory steps will be taken by the Legislature as fast as they can be. The people will be ready."
>
> "But," says the governor, "can it be gone through Congress without the Wilmot Proviso?"
>
> "Yes," says the senator, "the fanatics at the North could not get a corporal's guard against it."
>
> This conversation made a very great impression upon me at the time, so much so that I wrote it down, so as not to forget the language used, and it is from that copy my quote here.
>
> Whether the senator had secretly cherished the same purposes then, or whether he had formed them under the influence of the

intense excitement in Congress during the preceding year, created by the admission of California as a free state, I do not know, but we all know what his course was from that time on.

Mr. Gwin's statement that "the country was right for," had no foundation in fact. The country as a whole knew nothing about it, and those that were told were indifferent. But what he said about the course the Legislature would take, showed that he was well-informed on that point.

The Civil War was William's great undoing. Shortly after Abraham Lincoln's inauguration, William left Washington D.C. and traveled to Mississippi.

October 1861 From a perfectly reliable source we learned that ex-[California] Senator Gwin has burned his cotton crop in Mississippi, valued at $300,000 to keep it out of the hands of the government.

Twice in 1861, William was briefly jailed on suspicion of treason. Fearful of extended imprisonment, he left the country with his family in 1862 and took up residence in Paris where he contrived a scheme—with the backing of Napoleon III.

Napoleon wanted a French foothold in the Americas. William assured him that with sufficient military and financial support, he could persuade tens of thousands of Southerners and Californians to colonize the Sonora and Chihuahua provinces of Mexico for the French.

The plan required the cooperation of Mexico's Emperor Maximilian who was rightfully suspicious. By the fall of 1865, 60-year-old William realized his game plan was doomed and fled to Texas, then Louisiana soon after the Confederacy fell. He was captured and imprisoned by federal forces.

Eight months later, without explanation, William was released. He left for Paris immediately to reunite with his family and assimilate into the large community of Confederate expatriates. In 1867, with the return of his Democratic Party to power in California, William saw an opportunity to reclaim his life and re-enter politics.

In early 1868, the Gwins moved to San Francisco where William sold off what remained of his properties in California and Mississippi, and invested in quartz mines. The mines paid well and once again, he was a wealthy man. He joined the California State Democratic Club and involved himself in its activities.

In October 1875, a daughter of the late General Robert E. Lee was a guest at the Gwin home in San Francisco.

William died in New York on September 3, 1885, where he had gone for medical treatment. He was 80 years old. Believing his patient's positive attitude might improve his condition, the doctor decided not to tell William about the severity of his illness. His son traveled to New York to bring his remains home to California. The aggressive political demeanor had long-since faded. William was known by his family and friends as a genial person who would be missed.

27

William Morris Steuart

(Note to reader: authenticating research into the life of this delegate was hindered by the repeated misspelling of his last name—during his lifetime and by historians. Is it "u" or "w?" Steuart or Stewart? His christening announcement, and Last Will and Testament even identified him as Stewart while he signed his name at the Constitutional Convention as "Steuart.")

William was born on Oct 27, 1800, in Prince George's Parish Maryland to William and Margaret Steuart. There is no other verifiable information about his ancestry or early life. In 1820, a William M. Steuart was listed as a member of Harvard's elite Porcellian Club.

A reliable source wrote at the time that William arrived in California as secretary to the commodore of the U.S. Navy's Pacific Squadron, a group of marines and bluejacket sailors. This likely was Commodore John Sloat in July 1846. When William ran for Governor in November 1849, he added the prefix of colonel to his name.

William was in favor of organizing a provisional government in San Francisco. In January 1849, when the citizens of San Francisco elected delegates to attend the Provisional Government Convention, he received the highest number of votes. Yet, six months later the following notice appeared in the newspaper:

> The people of the District of San Francisco. Having been elected by the people of San Francisco a Justice of the Peace and subsequently appointed by the Legislative Assembly as President Judge of the Court of Appeals, the undersigned has diligently sought to discharge the duties imposed upon him; recent events making it doubtful whether the Municipal Government established by the people on 14 February last is sustained by a majority of our fellow citizens at the present time, the undersigned deems it does to himself and those who honored him with their suffrages to resign the high trusts reposed in him. William M Stewart, July 9, 1849

September 19. Mr. Steuart, a member from San Francisco, elect, appeared, was sworn, and took his seat.

Mr. Steuart. I am just recovering from a severe attack of illness, and it was only a short time since that I thought it would be at all practicable for me to take part in your deliberations. At the present moment I feel entirely incompetent to enter into this discussion, but I must beg leave to give one or two reasons which actuate me in the vote which I intend to give on this important question. Sir, I came to California from a State which has had no little experience in this matter. ...

... It is not my purpose, Mr. Chairman, to detain this assembly by entering into the troubles of that State on this subject ... I will content myself by merely stating that I have in my possession letters, received by the last steamer, from gentlemen prominent in the State of Maryland, informing me, and asking my advice as the effect, of their intention to come here in the spring with a large number of negroes, to be emancipated on the condition of serving them six or twelve months in the mines. ...

September 27. Mr. Steuart. I regret, very much, sir, that this clause has been introduced at all in the provisions of the Constitution. I need not say that I am always disposed to prevent an evil practice, and that I detest most heartily the practice of dueling; but I would be a hypocrite if I did not say that there are circumstances which compel men to resort to this mode of contest. I deem it entirely useless to attempt to restrain men by mere laws from engaging in duels, as long as they are not restrained by the general feeling of the community.

September 29. Mr. Steuart moved to amend the same by substituting therefor the following: Every white male citizen of the United States, and every white male inhabitant of California, as provided for under the treaty of peace exchanged and ratified at Queretaro, on the 30th day of May, 1848, of the age of 21 years, who shall have been a resident of the State six months next preceding the election, and the county and district in which he claims his vote thirty days, shall be entitled to vote at all elections which are now, or hereafter may be authorized by law.

Following the Constitutional Convention, William and three other delegates spoke to a crowd of over 1,000 in Sacramento on the outcome of the historic gathering in Monterey. William was nominated for governor but not elected. He then ran for city council and was elected; but when he ran for mayor, he was not elected.

The 1850 federal census listed him as living in Benicia as a practicing attorney.

In November 1862, William is mentioned in a newspaper article as being in Carson City Nevada offering subscription books for the Union Pacific Railroad. A short time later, the Nevada Territorial Legislature elected a new representative to replace William.

As a founding member of the Society of California Pioneers, he served as Marshall at the organization's third anniversary of California's admission into the Union on September 10, 1863.

How and why William returned to the East Coast is not known. Could it have anything to do with what happened at the first legislative session held in San Jose in April 1850? The bill to change the names of the towns of Pleasant Valley and Steuart was read for the third time and passed.

In 1863, William was living with his sister Helen in Washington D.C. In August 1865, the 65-year-old married 34-year-old Laura L. Berry. In the 1870 federal census, Col. William Steuart listed his occupation as a lawyer.

In November 1872, 72-year-old William knew he was dying and dictated his Last Will and Testament, appointing his "beloved wife" Laura L. Steuart as the executrix of his estate. His sister Helen is mentioned as a beneficiary, "to share and share alike."

28

Alfred James Ellis

Alfred was born in September 1816 in Oneida County New York. A New England Seamen's Protection Certificate No. 30 was issued on April 9, 1834, to 17-year-old James Ellis. His seaman's life took him to the South Pacific, living for a while in New Zealand, then Hawaii where he found a wife. In June 1847, he arrived in San Francisco aboard the brig *Francisca* with his wife and three-month-old daughter who would live only six more months.

Alfred purchased an adobe near the end of Montgomery Street. After converting it into a boarding house and groggery, the establishment became a favorite of sailors and master mariners.

Alfred's respectability in the community was further enhanced in January 1848 when the San Francisco Town Council confirmed him as the town treasurer, "whose duty it shall be to receive, safely keep, and disperse all monies belonging to the town."

There was nothing controversial or biased in Alfred's remarks at the Constitutional Convention.

September 12. Mr. Ellis thought one more provision ought to be introduced—that all single men should be married in three months.

October 12. On motion of Mr. Ellis, it was unanimously Resolved, That a committee of three be appointed to transmit a copy of the Constitution of the State of California to General Riley, acting Governor of California, with an accompanying letter signed by the President of this body, requesting the Governor to forward the same to the President of the United States by the earliest opportunity. The Chair appointed Messrs, Ellis, Hastings, and McCarver as such committee.

Over the next 33 years, Alfred's name appeared so frequently in the local newspapers that reading the clippings in their chronological order seems like the best way to present the rest of his life story.

February 1850 The undersigned gives notice that he will leave for the United States on 1 March next. All persons having demands against him are requested to present them and those indebted to him are solicited to call and settle immediately, ... A.J. Ellis

March 1850 To rent—the fine dwelling house now occupied by A.J. Ellis Esq. with the furniture complete. Possession given first of March. Inquire of Haight & Wadsworth, office in the old Portsmouth house.

March 1852 We regret to hear from the messenger that Hon. A.J. Ellis, member of the [state] assembly from this country, was injured by falling from the head of a flight of stairs on Monday night at the Osborne house. He was lodging at this house and arose in the night to go downstairs. Mistaking the open stairway for the landing, he stepped off and fell to the bottom, badly bruising his head and face.

August 1852 Among the passengers on the Golden Gate, we are happy to welcome the return of Mr. AJ Ellis one of our old and prominent citizens who has been on a visit to the Atlantic states. Notwithstanding the great amount of sickness on the Isthmus, they have fortunately escaped and return in excellent health and fine spirits.

Sept 1852 A trotting and pacing match, came off yesterday on the Pioneer Course between TK Battles's trotter, and A.J. Ellis's pacer. A large number of the gentry had collected on the spot to witness the sport.

January 1853 The concert of Miss Kate Hayes last evening was an elegant affair. There could not have been less than one hundred and fifty ladies in the house. The singing was admirable as it always is and the concert yielded the handsome sum of $1250 for the orphans of the city. The next six concerts of Miss Hayes are "subscription." The drawing for the choice of seats took place this morning. The best seats in the house were secured by AJ Ellis.

March 1853 For sale or rent—in a central part of this city, two brick cottages, well calculated for residences for small families.

One of the above is well furnished with everything necessary for housekeeping, and the furniture will be sold cheap as the owner is about to leave for the east. Apply to AJ Ellis.

January 1854 The Goliath arrived the last evening and brought the news of the disaster of the "Golden Gate." The Golden Gate went on shore on the reef just outside of the harbor of San Diego at 3 PM. Soon after she struck she made a signal of distress and the Goliath went to her assistance as soon as possible, making two attempts to tow her off. One of the most terrible southeast gales which has taken place for many years sprung up, compelling the Goliath for her own safety and those on board to put back and leave the Golden Gate and all on board to the mercy of an all wise providence. ... The Goliath brought up about two hundred passengers and two hundred and thirty-four mail bags. ... Among the passengers we noticed the name of AJ Ellis of the city.

May 1855 Organization of the Jockey Club. The meeting was held last evening ... at the St. Nicholas Hotel for the purpose of organizing a Jockey Club in the city and establishing racing and other sporting matters upon a more elevated and legitimate basis. Mr. AJ Ellis was called to the chair. About thirty of the prominent sporting gentlemen of San Francisco were present.

March 1856 Died ... in San Francisco March 18, Thomas son of AJ Ellis, aged 10 years and 6 months.

July 1857 John Burns, Patrick Daily and Jacob Chase were tried yesterday on a charge of disturbing the peace, in the nighttime, at a saloon on Montgomery Street. Mr. P Hunt testified that on

Friday night, between twelve and 1 o'clock he stopped into the saloon and saw a man named James Ganon strike at and clinch with Mr. AJ Ellis; they tumbled upon the floor. A witness called upon the defendants to assist in separating the combatants, but instead of doing so they pushed him away and swore he should not interfere. They tried to encourage the fight all they could and one of them even went so far as to catch a pitcher off the counter and attempt to strike Mr. Ellis. Mr. George Alexander, one of the proprietors of the saloon, also testified to the attack upon Mr. Ellis and the abusive words of the defendants, and in general riotous conduct on that occasion; that Mr. Ellis tried to avoid the difficulty, but could not, and the defendants showed an anxiety to fight and disturb the quiet of the neighborhood. There was an abundance of witnesses present in the courtroom ready to testify, but they were not needed. ...

Nov 1859 Lost—on the 28th by the undersigned, a small POCKET MEMORANDUM BOOK, containing papers of value to the owner only. The finder will be suitably rewarded by leaving the above at my office, over Parrott & Company's Bank, corner Sacramento and Montgomery streets. AJ Ellis

August 1861 Yesterday a match was made for a purse of $1000, between AJ Ellis and Charles Hosmer and W D Chapman, to run their horses under the saddle to San Mateo, 22 miles. The race was won by Chapman in one hour and fifteen minutes.

Nov 13, 1861 Divorce filed: Ellis, Mary A. vs Ellis, Alfred J.

Feb. 1865 The San Francisco Bulletin of February 21 makes

the following exhibit in the above connection: the records of the Internal Revenue Department for the first California district, comprising the counties of San Francisco and San Mateo, show that between fifteen thousand and sixteen thousand persons are in receipt of incomes exceeding the amount legally exempted. This district probably contains no more than 120,000 souls and is credited with the possession of property assessed at only $85,078,658; yet it yields a taxable income of $14,500,000.

Without further comments, for which we lack space at present, we present here with the list of one hundred seventy-six names, on parties paying an income tax on two thousand dollars or upwards, in this district, showing who are our wealthiest citizens: Mrs. AJ Ellis: $10,000

Feb 1872 LOST pocket book containing Certificate No. 93..100 shares Alpha, Certificate No. 10618..10 shares Savage, Certificate No. 920..100 shares Phoenix (silver mine), Certificate No. 930..100 shares Phoenix, Also, two notes, $500 each, at sixty and ninety days respectively, in my favor and endorsed. Handsome competence will be paid the finder. AJ Ellis

April 1872 The Stock Market continues its great strength and activity, more especially in the Comstock (silver) mines. On the day following the recent election of officers for the Phoenix Company several of the gentlemen resigned and others were elected. The board stands now as follows: ... AJ Ellis

May 1876 AJ Ellis and others have sold to BF Morrow the lot 137-1/2 x 137-1/2, on the southeast corner of California and Battery streets for $320,000.

<u>April 1877</u> Owing to an unusually heavy gale of wind which blew constantly from the West yesterday, there was but a small attendance at the Bay District courses to witness the racing on the bill for the day. The first race was the two-mile trotting contest. … The race was a good one, being well contested throughout. The judges' stand was occupied by WK Graham, AJ Ellis and Mr. C Crocker.

The 1880 San Francisco census listed Alfred as 63 years old, single, a boarder, his occupation speculator. He died at the age of 66 on July 18, 1883, in San Francisco, and was buried the next day.

PART VI

San Joaquin District

29

John McHenry Hollingsworth

John was born on February 11, 1823, in Baltimore Maryland, the third of nine children. His maternal great-grandfather, Samuel Chase, represented the state of Maryland when he placed his signature on the Declaration of Independence.

In *The Journal of Lieutenant John McHenry Hollingsworth*, we learn that John was 23 years old in August 1846 when he was mustered into service as a brevet lieutenant in [future fellow-delegate] Edward Shannon's company of the New York Volunteers and put aboard the *Susan Drew*. (The reader may recall that the packet ship sailed around the Cape Horn on its way to San Francisco, a distance of 13,225 miles.)

- … I do not like the sea. If ever I can get to land once more I shall never leave it. You never feel well at sea …

- … a butterfly came on board—had I been on shore I should not have looked at it.

- I cannot write the vessel shakes so much. …

- How glad I am that I do not use tobacco; how much money I can save by not using it. It is well that I have a good Mother, with God's help I will follow her counsel. I believe she never forgets me in her prayers, how much trouble have I given her and how often have I grieved her and my sisters.

- How bad I feel today, I have never felt well since I left home. A farmer's life is the easiest one in the world and the best for health; it has spoilt me and made me unfit for anything else.

- The harmony of our mess was broken for the first time today. Liquor was the cause of it. What a curse it is, I wish that there was none. I have been brought up better. Thanks to a kind Mother I trust I may be preserved from it. How many fine young men are throwing themselves away by their folly. I would do anything to persuade Ned not to tamper with it. I hope when I see him again that he will be wiser.

- Mutiny is among us. The men of Company D were ordered to bathe, which they refused to do. ...Captain Shannon detailed some men ...to carry the order into execution. By some mistake all the men were composed of new recruits, they mutinied also, and they were sent to the guard house with the rest of the mutineers.

- The guard house is full, when will this end. Retired to bed early. Was wakened by a great noise. The officer of the guard told me that he could not manage the prisoners. That they had broken down the door of the guard house, were out and tearing the house to pieces. ... The guard on the forecastle assisted the mutineers to throw the plank over board, they cheered long and loud.

- It now began to spread more. The rest of the men who had behaved well hitherto now joined in the cheering. ... There are too many gentleman soldiers with us; they are the cause of all our difficulties.

- How tired I am of the Ship and of the sea life.

- We will cross the line to day. Neptune cannot come on board, we are too strong for him.

- I sometimes, think that I ought not to have become a soldier, how much I have got to learn. I must study hard. How much I have neglected. How often I feel mortified, but it has been part of my life to conceal my ignorance. I will strive hard and I must not be so down hearted. It is all my own fault. ... They think at home that I never tried. But I never was blest with intellect like any other person. I have always had a very indolent mind. But I shall improve I hope some of these days. I will not mortify my family if ever it is God's will that I see them again.

- The more I see of a sailor's life the more I dislike it. They are a set of tyrants. Their greatest pleasure is to tell you a lie of some kind, and then say they have quizzed you....You can never find out on land, what a sailor is.

- I am glad I am not on the Court Martial. They wanted to put me on as Judge Advocate; they do not know how stupid I am, I am not competent to be one. I do not think there is an Officer on board that does not wish himself at home, they will never volunteer again. A vessel is no place for soldiers, it does not suit them, it was bad policy to send us by sea. You cannot have any discipline. I think if one were shot it would bring them to their senses.

- I never was as careless as I now am in my dress. I have paid no attention to shaving and I do not think I ever looked so homely as I do now when I look in the glass. I do not know myself I hope I will fatten up before I get back.

- I am so tired of the sea, that I often go to the pigpen and look at the pigs eating and wish myself at home feeding some of ours.

- Weather very cold and stormy, all have colds—spend half of our time in bed—…Some of the officers have had severe falls and been much hurt—It is owing to the decks being so wet—

- The weather is very cool and has been so for the last ten days with a sea running mountains high and rain, making us all keep our beds—we have done nothing else but eat and sleep for some time—in fact cannot keep ourselves warm unless we go to bed—extremes of weather, much arguing amongst themselves, drunkenness, …

- Many of our officers as well as myself have regretted our coming out here while the war has been carried on in the enemy's country and we so far from the scene of strife. On hearing of General Scott's advance upon the City of Mexico — we wished we had been in the States to have joined him—We have done nothing and long for an opportunity of distinguishing or extinguishing ourselves.

- [After arriving in San Francisco] I must now pack for Monterey. I am sorry to leave the Susan Drew. I have been so long in her and seen a good deal. ... I have got so used to the hard bread and biscuit that I prefer it to any other—and the water that I made so much fuss about at the first part of my voyage I now drink off without thinking about it. ...

- I went to a fandango last night and enjoyed myself very much looking on as I did not dance—I have not been introduced to a single lady since I got here—This dance was nothing in comparison to the great Navy ball.

- We have made arrangements for having a fandango weekly—I saw General Castro's little son at the last ball—he was asked if he would not like to be in the army and fight the Mexicans—he spoke out very boldly and said, "No but I would like to fight the Americans and drive them from the country." He is only twelve years of age and the enemies of his country were around him but he spoke fearlessly—His father is now trying to raise troops to march against us. ...

- Been much engaged trying to be transferred to the G Company—succeeded at last.

- Arrived at San Pedro—landed, pitched our tents and made a wharf. Did not know till we were done that it was Sunday. Will march to Los Angeles tomorrow, distant 25 miles. San Pedro situated on the coast consists of two houses, not a tree or blade of grass near it. It is all one vast plain, neither wood or water, all our water is brought from the vessel in canteens.

- Walked over to [the home of] Don Luis—met a large party of ladies. Spent a pleasant time—Had the band there, gave them some music. Rode the Colonel's horse home. Saw a beautiful Spanish girl there, gave her a bouquet, and murdered Spanish at her at a great rate.

- Been visiting. Had some pleasant evenings. Saw Mrs. General Flores at Don Luis. She is a very interesting woman. The most popular house is Mr. [Abel] Stearns. He has married a young Spanish girl but the principal attraction is [her sister] Senorita Isidora Bandini. The lady I met at Don Luis. She is a great belle and a great flirt… I must now stop but perhaps Isidora you will again come on these pages.

- Walked over to see Isidora last night. It was Sunday and I had nothing to do. I found her looking lovely as ever. I was told there would be a dance at 10 o'clock and requested to be there. I was anxious to know if Isidora would dance on Sunday. I was one of the last who arrived. Ah Isidora you are but a heathen. She is dancing with one of Kearney's dark mustachoed dragoons. She was dressed in a plain white muslin and had left off all those hateful Spanish ornaments, and wore nothing in her hair but a beautiful rose I had presented her with that evening.

- Everyone was seeking her for a partner. She never looked so lovely. It had long been wondered who was the favoured admirer. Some said the Marines, some thought the Dragoons. Yes Reader, smile not at what I now tell you. Say not it was my vanity, but believe me when I assert that I had long known, that the 2d Lieutenant of the Volunteers [Hollingsworth himself] was preferred to all.—I took my place behind the dancers in a retired part of the room, and felt as if I had done wrong in coming on Sunday to a dance.

- I watched Isidora for some time. She did not seem to dance with her usual animation. She seemed looking for someone anxiously. Her eyes often wandered round the room and I began to feel jealous. At last I caught her eye and a bright glance it was. It told me I was the absent one, she looked for. A moment before, and I had felt neglected by all the world. I had been drooping in spirit for some time. But now I felt a confidence I had never known before. How I longed to lead her to the dance, but that could not be for I did not know how.

- She seemed hurt that I did not ask her to dance and sent to ask me to waltze with her. It was in vain I assured her that I did not know how and at last came over and sat down by me. I told her I did not know how. She said she would teach me. I at last asked her to dance the next set with her. She promised to help me all she could. I led her out and …presented my left hand first. I got through at last. She insisted I did very well, but I knew better. She now took her seat by my side instead of dancing. I got many dark looks and the dragoon took his hat and walked off. Ah Isadora you were the cause of my first dance. I must now take leave of this fair one and go on duty as officer of guard.

- Just returned from San Pedro and reported myself at headquarters. Been absent one week.

- Got the blues very bad indeed in consequence of Isidora having jilted me. She appears to have forgotten me entirely during my short absence.

- Went to Mr. Sale's last evening, Isidora was there, seemed to want to make up. Don't intend to let her.

- Gave the people here a splendid ball. Everything passed off well, except a little difficulty—I was much mortified that I could not waltze with her. She is the most perfect coquette I ever saw. She was dressed in a rich pink and gold silk, with a shawl on worth $300! I never saw her look better. I was in full uniform and entered with her on my arm. She was the belle of the evening. Went to take leave of Isidora. She is going to the country. We parted good friends. She gave me a … parting gift.

- [Isadora] has been very sick. Dr. Griffin has been trying to cure her eyes that a quack has nearly put out. I went to see her last evening and was sitting at the window when her mother came in. She did not seem to like my being there talking to her daughter poor girl; she does not know that she has a God or that she has a soul to be saved. She has a drunken father and her mother is the worst of women.

- I have again had a long talk with Kit Carson — He dined with me to day. He spoke of the different expeditions that he went on with Fremont and gave me many particulars of those trips—the hardships and difficulties that Fremont has never mentioned. He said, "The government can never repay me for my trouble." He has promised to visit me when he returns to the United States—I hope that something may turn up so that I may return with him.

- Carson called on me today—I had a long talk with him—he told me of his first entry in a room filled with ladies; he said he never was so frightened in his life—Yes the hero of a hundred fights was scared at a room filled with ladies.

- Colonel Burton has had another fight at La Paz and given the Mexicans a sound thrashing—Captains Steel and Nagle have distinguished themselves—the latter is now under arrest by order of Colonel Mason for shooting two prisoners that were taken in a fight—Captain Nagle's conduct has been disapproved of by all; in fact, his whole course since he has been in California has been marked by cold-blooded acts of cruelty.

- I was on guard duty—It was Sunday and crowds of persons were walking on the heights, the day was beautiful, our band was present playing some beautiful airs—I had a visit from a number of ladies among whom was the fair Isadora—I invited them in to the guard room and shewed them all the attention I could.

- We received the news that one thousand men were wanted at Mazatlan to garrison the places our navy had taken possession of—This news was hailed with joy by our regiment as we thought we had the best right to go and were much disappointed to hear that Governor Mason had sent Major Hardy to Oregon for a battalion of Mormons to go down—and Lieutenant Warner was dispatched to the Salt Lake for the same purpose—we all think the Mormons will not go but will have no objection to garrison this place while we go—Should we have the good fortune to go we all think it is a step nearer home.

- I have neglected to note down many occurrences of late and this is the first time I have opened my journal for many days—there is however but little stirring. [Kit] Carson is making preparations to leave this country for the United States and we are all grumbling at our hard fate in not being permitted to go with him—We have parades every day, duty is harder now than ever—the battalion paraded in white pants this morning in the public square and looked well.

- Received letters from home urging my return ...

- A theatre is to open here on the fourth of July—We

shall have some fine acting—I often wile away an evening at it.

- News of the wealth of the gold region has reached here.

- Went to work today and settled every bill and am glad to be able to say out of debt, but for the first time since I left home without money! It would be unfortunate for me to be disbanded at this time for I should not then have the smallest chance of returning home—My life has been prosperous so far since I reached here and I hope a dark cloud is not gathering over me—Things appear to be getting gloomy at this post—Our men are deserting rapidly after they have been paid off and the news of the immense quantities of gold that is found in the mining district is a great inducement for them to desert. We have lost eight men from one company and a rush was made yesterday by the prisoners and three of them escaped.

- Don Pio Pico has arrived from Mexico and claims the right of Governor of California — He has refused to report to Colonel Stevenson and Lieutenant Bonnycastle was sent last night to arrest him as a spy but failed to find him—He (Pico) however sent word early this morning that he would give himself up today.... There is no officer in command of the dragoons and unless Lieutenant D returns tonight I shall be assigned to duty with that Corps—I live in the barracks with them now having charge of the public funds. It is a post of great responsibility for the Californians are more disposed for a revolt now than they ever have been—Pico is stirring them up and the Sonorians have sworn to attack the barracks and take the iron chest that belongs to the Government. They shall have a hard fight for it for I have it now safe in the room with me.

- Colonel Mason has sent an order for Lieutenant S of the dragoons to proceed with a party and one volunteer officer to the gold region—The post of second in command was offered to me but I declined it after much reflection—I thought it would be imprudent in my going at this sickly season of the year into that district ... I hope I shall not regret that I did not embrace the opportunity of visiting the gold regions for I need all the money I can raise—I have paid my debts and owe no man anything but must say I have very little money left—God only knows how I am to get home.

- I asked today for leave of absence from the post for a day—it was refused me. I did not want to be excused from duty for I was not on duty but I have never had one day's leave of absence yet, without some hesitation on the part of Colonel S—my object in getting leave of absence was to go in the country some miles to purchase mules to go home on but as usual I have had bad luck—I have had nothing else of late—I thought things would not go on so fair for me much longer—Things appear dark for me now, darker than they have ever been before.

- August 17, 1848 Received the first official news of Peace.

- August 23. Commenced making preparations for the gold mines.

- "FAREWELL TO LOS ANGELES" Sad is my heart! not poor pile of adobies because I am leaving thee, exchanging thy poor exterior for the bright looks of our own fine marble, brick and wooden edifices, but because of the bright eyes and warm hearts of the sunny smiled maids, your cheerless exterior hides—First to the Dona A-a whose innocent laughing mode of addressing the "teniente alto," will long be remembered with feelings of mingled joy and sadness—Joy that I have ever possessed so much of thy esteem and friendship, sadness that our lots in this world should have been cast so widely apart—I bid a long a tender farewell, and sincerely do I pray that yours may be a life of happiness uncrossed by pain or care—Next dear Senorita Isidora, but alas why name I thee so soon? why not defer to the last what I so much dread and hate—still like medicine, in one bold draught and all is o'er—to thee must I bid adieu—God had predetermined that our fates should not be linked and 'twere vain by hopes or wishes endeavour his decree revoke, as lover, faithful have I been to thee, since first we met, and now that the mandate has gone forth which separates us for ever, believe me dear one, thy image shall ever hold in my heart a foremost place In sadness and in Joy, alike, will I recall thy sweet and tender glances, linked with the memory of thy softly lisped endearments and fervently pray for your happiness—...McH. H.—

- We were soon ready and off, leaving the city rather in a

ludicrous manner. The Colonel was mounted on a beautiful horse which he could not manage and as sundry of our mules were getting rid of their loads, the Colonel's horse seemed anxious to get rid of his too. I soon found out that many of our party did not know how to ride. Our friends on all sides wished us a pleasant journey, and we raised a cloud of dust as we passed through the town. I rode by the side of Colonel Stevenson on my beautiful gray charger arching his neck and stepping proudly, as if he was aware of the white handkerchiefs that waved to the rider a farewell from the windows.

(Gold mining didn't pan out so well, then this.)

- In those few days I suffered, I think, everything — hunger and cold, the constant dread of Indians and wild beasts. One day when we ventured to make a little fire, the explosion of some cartridges nearly put out my eyes, and caused me great suffering. We were then lost on the great plain. I have left out much that was interesting in this trip, for want of time, and have only written that, which would most interest my friends, should this book ever come to their hands. Suffice it now to say that a few more days of such suffering would have ended my days in this world.

- AUG. 17, 1849. I once more take my pen in hand having skipped over the last five months of my life. I have again passed over the San Joaquin Valley the scene of my former hardships and explored still further into the placers. And I now again have returned to Monterey

The Delegates of 1849

resolved to go home. I lost all by a fire in the mines. I must now return home a poor man.

John apparently made an impression on the voters in the San Joaquin District while he was there. They elected him a delegate to the Constitutional Convention without his having done any campaigning.

He was the only delegate from the San Joaquin District to be present on the first day of the Convention. Throughout the entire six weeks, the only mention of his name is in the voting roll call. John need not worry how he was to return to the U.S. After the Convention adjourned, General Riley selected him as the bearer of the new Constitution to the Government at Washington.

(Extract From New York Mirror.) Among the arrivals are ... Lieutenant John McHenry Hollingsworth, late of the 1st New York Regiment of Volunteers. ... and ...bearer of the new Constitution to the President of the United States, together with official dispatches to the War Department—a mark of confidence of which many an older officer might well be proud. Lieutenant Hollingsworth leaves California, warmly esteemed by all who knew him, and with the best wishes for his future welfare.

After distinguishing himself to the president and the War Department, John was appointed the Georgetown collector for the Chesapeake and Ohio Canal, a position he filled satisfactorily for quite some time.

He also indulged in matrimony. In November 1865, 42-year-old John married 40-year-old Virginia Nicholls. It is believed this was the first marriage for each of them.

In 1872, John was appointed the superintendent of George Washington's grand Mount Vernon estate along the Potomac, a position ideally suited to his gregarious personality. In 1858, the Mount Vernon Ladies Association acquired the estate from the Washington family and have been responsible for maintaining the property ever since. No doubt the ladies were sad to see the elegant gentleman leave when John retired in 1885.

John died from Bright's Disease on April 15, 1889, at the age of 66 and was buried in Oak Hill Cemetery, Washington D.C.

30

James McHall Jones

James's obituary refers to Iberville Louisiana as being the home of his family and his exceptional social qualifications. Is it any wonder when the parish describes itself as "Tucked between the swamps of the Atchafalaya and the bustling state capital of Baton Rouge is a parish rich with legend and mystery, where tales of survival and triumph are central to its core."

The truth is, James was born in Georgetown Kentucky ("a small town bursting with charm") on December 31, 1823. Information from a renown genealogy website indicates his mother was 15 years old when James was born, that his father had died and his mother remarried to Dr. Joseph Hornsby when she was 28 years old.

The family moved to Plaquemine Louisiana where Dr. Hornsby set up his medical practice, and Mrs. Hornsby aspired passionately to transform 13-year-old James into a fine southern gentleman with many redeeming qualities and excellent social standing.

James's education consisted of reading the law to enter the bar, which he did at age 20 in 1843. He worked in private practice for two years in Plaquemine, then traveled to Paris, supposedly for more study and exposure to refined society.

During his two years abroad, he mastered French, Italian and Spanish, collected an extensive library of European law books, and enjoyed dancing, fencing, boxing and drawing lessons. He also sought out the most excellent remedies for tuberculosis, a disease he contracted in his late teens, the same time as his mother. Foremost among his treatments were daily doses of opium.

The primary benefit of opium is to relieve or suppress pain. It may also induce a state of euphoria or other enhanced moods. This might explain James's descriptions in his letters to his mother of his near-heroic accomplishments. A critical physiological effect with opium is suppression of the cough reflex, the telltale giveaway of the disease, making it possible for James to appear healthy. The habitual use of opium, however, produces physical and mental deterioration and shortens life. James was no exception.

His valiant adventures in Europe no doubt made it difficult for him to settle back into life as a country lawyer after he returned to Plaquemine. California beckoned and with his mother's blessing he set sail in July 1849, boarding the U.S. mail steamship *Falcon* at New Orleans where he made the acquaintance of fellow Southerner, William Gwin. Finding an eager pupil, Gwin likely educated James on the opportunities that awaited such a bright and enthusiastic young man in California.

Hearing about the upcoming Constitutional Convention when he landed in San Francisco, James jumped into action. With only a week to canvass, he made his way from San Francisco to the southern mining camps, stopping gold diggers on the trail and escorting them to the polls. His efforts were successful; the newcomer gained a seat at the Convention.

In late August, James wrote his mother yet another exalting letter.

> I have made the warmest personal friends of those who command the Convention, the government and the trade. I can bring a great influence to support them, and they support me. I am the originator of a commission to be named by convention for the purpose of codifying all the law. It is an idea that must succeed; and I will be at its head with an income of about seven thousand more or less per year. I have been consulted, too, by persons high in authority if I would accept a seat on the supreme bench at the time of our formation as a state. I will not if it interferes with the commission; for I consider the honor of originating and presiding at the formation of an entire system of laws, quite equal to that of U.S. Senator. ... All this is the fruit of some little skill in playing political cards ...

It seems James also came to the Convention with an attitude:

> September 3. Mr. Jones considered it a poor privilege, to which every prisoner at the bar was entitled, that of defending his rights. He did not come here to subject himself to the discretion of any committee. He came to represent a large and respectable constituency, by whom he was elected, and he claimed a seat in this Convention, not as a matter of sympathy, but as a matter of right. His reputation, he trusted was above committees. In the absence of full election returns, he contended that the word of a gentleman who was deemed worthy of the confidence reposed in him by his constituents was sufficient to establish his right to a seat in this Convention — at least until the arrival of complete returns. Mr. Jones proceeded at some length to sustain the position which he had assumed.

September 12. Mr. Jones. I am merely referring, Mr. President, to that general rule which protects members of a parliamentary body from gross and insulting remarks from any member. I rise to claim the protection of the House from such remarks, and, I believe, the first thing to be done is to require the Secretary to put those remarks down. I call upon the Secretary to put them down.

October 10. Mr. Jones. I had the particular good fortune, sir, to obtain the floor this morning before any other member of the Convention. I call it a particular good fortune, for I have no doubt if any member had known that I wished to obtain the floor, there would have been some difficulty in getting it, I made a motion, sir, to reconsider the last vote of the House on this subject; and I gave notice that if the reconsideration prevailed, I would offer the proposition which I hold in my hand. It was for that purpose that I moved the reconsideration; ...

The third-highest number of times a delegate's name is mentioned in the Convention transcript falls to James Hall: 237 mentions, most often in connection with a motion, several to reconsider a vote.

After the Constitutional Convention, James moved to San Jose where he set up a partnership law practice whose cases involved litigation over land titles. His clients had little money; fees were paid with interest in real property. James acquired several parcels and mortgages.

In September 1850, he was offered an appointment as a United

States district attorney and turned it down because the salary was too low.

On December 23, 1850, James was nominated by President Millard Fillmore to a new seat on the U.S. District Court for the Southern District of California. He accepted the career-fulfilling position but would hold it for only one year.

His new life was just beginning when he received word that his mother had died of tuberculosis. He immediately recessed his court and traveled to Louisiana for her funeral. When he returned to Los Angeles several weeks later, he was a changed man, considerably more somber. He executed his Last Will and Testament, leaving everything to his step-siblings, ages seven and nine. In October, he was baptized into the Roman Catholic faith. On December 1, he adjourned his court. On December 15, 1851, he died from complications of tuberculosis, not yet 28 years old.

31

Benjamin Franklin Moore

Benjamin was born in 1824 at Moore's Bluff Alabama. The site became known as Moore's Bluff when Benjamin's father, Thomas Moore, a settler from Tennessee, built a cabin there in 1815. Located along the Tombigbee River, the town was an important trading point for cotton. During the early 1800s, thousands of bales were shipped each year.

Benjamin came to California in 1848, likely as a veteran of the Mexican-American War, calling himself Colonel Moore when he entered politics. He also called himself a lawyer, although he had no credentials. He did have a shrewd insight into human nature and established a law practice in Sonora Tuolumne County. He specialized in criminal law, representing the accused, and relied on others to write his legal documents.

He knew better than to bluff the real lawyers at the Constitutional Convention, where he identified himself as a "gentleman of elegant leisure." He was also known as the most disagreeable man at the Convention, acting half-drunk most of the time, which made the enormous Bowie knife he carried at his side appear more ominous. However disagreeable he was, his recorded remarks do not reflect any hostility.

September 12. Mr. Moore hoped his friend (Mr. Jones) would not require any apology here. If there was any misunderstanding, let it be settled out of doors. He (Mr. Moore) would not trouble the House, if insulted, by asking any apology here.

October 2. Mr. Moore. I have merely to say that there has been a great deal of debate here for nothing. No man in the House doubts that the Government of the United States has collected money that they had no right to collect, and that the money is in the hands of its officers. I can see no harm in claiming what belongs to the people of California.

What was really going on with Benjamin's disagreeable nature and being half-drunk? Sixteen years later he would be committed to the Stockton Insane Asylum—terminally ill and emotionally unstable. Had his illness already taken hold when he came to the Convention, and the liquor was his attempt at self-medicating?

Following adjournment of the Constitutional Convention, Benjamin likely resumed his precarious law practice—and fell in love. On February 9, 1857, he married Mary McCarthy. The couple would have two children.

In December 1861, it was announced that the "Pacific Guard," a new military company, was organized at Dutch Flat, Placer County, and a B. F. Moore was its Captain.

By December 1865, Benjamin was a very sick man—in body, mind, and spirit.

Committed to Stockton State Hospital by the probate judge. Married and has two children, the youngest four years, occupation lawyer. The window of insanity is trying to kill himself, fears starvation of himself and his family versus best friends are his worst enemies, probably inclined to injure others. This attack appeared three months ago, it became marked and appeared to some extent for months before; this is not the first; disease increasing; is generally rational on many subjects, has no insane relatives, very sensitive and peculiar in many respects. Has failed in physical health to some extent; cause of insanity, dyspepsia (impaired digestion); class, incipient mania—no treatment. Admitted December 23rd, 1865. Friends will pay. Died January 2nd, 1866 at age 45 of uremic poisoning, consequent upon disease of the kidneys.

32

Benjamin S. Lippincott

Benjamin was born on October 6, 1815, in New York, New York into a family of prosperous merchant/grocers. In 1846 he left New York and traveled to Independence Missouri where he joined the Boggs/Morin train of 69 wagons headed for California. He would ride in a wagon with other bachelors, have their mule team stolen and have to use slower-moving oxen, be shot with an arrow in the lower leg by attacking Indians (and pull it through himself), and before arriving at Sutter's Fort, come down with camp fever that would incapacitate him for two miserable weeks.

Once healthy and mobile, he wasted no time in establishing his mercantile business, purchasing items in Yerba Buena and selling them to customers farther inland. He was making a good profit; then he heard about John Fremont and his California Battalion. In a letter to his brother-in-law Ezek, dated March 22, 1847, Benjamin wrote:

> What brought me amongst them (Fremont's Battalion) is simply this, while selling a small consignment of goods at the head of San Francisco Bay, a messenger came with a request from Colonel Fremont to proceed to Yerba Buena (the New York of California) and there procure a canon, ammunition etc. and deliver it to an officer who, in the meantime, would arrive at the head of the bay.
>
> On my return with the gun, my feelings were listed for the cause and I proceeded with the escort to Camp St. John's, one hundred, twenty miles south. Here Fremont attended me a Lieutenancy in Company H which I accepted and from that time on was in more perilous service than any other company, constantly as the advance guard, except when on a horse racing expedition. With a detachment of ten, I succeeded in taking three prisoners and they were the first to be brought in camp in the campaign. So here am I now about six hundred miles south of San Francisco hail, hearty and busy. So long as good pay, so long am I here. [From descriptions in his letters, Benjamin was not a robust man when he left New York, and he later credits California's climate with giving him good health.]

Following his release from the California Battalion, Benjamin wasted no time in making his fortune, as he explained in another letter to his brother-in-law Ezek on February 6, 1847:

> I have in my possession an article from Thomas Larkin former counsel and the best merchant in the country, guaranteeing to raise and put in my possession $4,000 which amount I am to invest in goods at the Sandwich Islands. The appointment of assistant quartermaster [on a sailing ship] has been offered to me. But I wish only to remain in employ temporarily. ...
>
> My letter of introduction has been of the utmost importance to me. At once been made acquainted with all the prominent businessmen of the country. The amount due me from government and funds and property on hand amounts to not less than $900. Mr.

Larkin is now building a large store and warehouse at Yerba Buena which will be open for a produce in general assortment store.

In a letter to his sister Amelia, dated October 1, 1849 he wrote:

> ... My prospects are the same as when I last wrote home. My business in the mines has proved lucrative and my investments in land good. We have removed the seat of government to San Jose where fortunately I owned thirty-one lots which only advanced twenty percent. I sold my last lot in San Francisco on September 1st, which cost me four hundred dollars – for two thousand dollars. This I have reinvested.
>
> You will soon hear of a new town called Eureka which I have the honor of locating and having surveyed. It is situated in my district near the Southern mines.

During the entire Constitutional Convention, Benjamin did not rise to comment, make a motion or disagree. In November 1849, October 1850, September 1855, and November 1860 he was elected to the California legislature, as assemblyman and senator and nearly became lieutenant governor. In a letter to his sister Amelia, dated January 26, 1851, written from the Senate chamber:

> We allow mister vanity to say a little about himself. I think I see you nod assent. You must know our Governor Burnett resigned some two weeks ago and the Lieutenant Governor McDougal installed as Governor, consequently a Lieutenant Governor as President of the Senate was wanted. There were many aspirants in our body. I declined the nomination, but received a majority of the votes. I then requested each member not to support me. ...
>
> Much feeling exists here between Northerners and Southerners. This ultra radicalian I despise, particularly a fanatical Southerner.
>
> ... I have been thinking seriously of making a flying trip home

this spring – circumstances will govern – and desirous of seeing you all. What would you say to an hombre weighing about 186 pounds, hardy and hale, stalk in among you someday … I feel the same buoyancy of spirits as when I was eighteen. My health is excellent. The climate suits me.

In 1860, Benjamin did return to New Jersey, probably by way of Panama, considering what he wrote in the letter to Ezek about not wanting to repeat the overland journey.

On March 5, 1867, 52-year-old Benjamin married 48-year-old Louisa Cutter. The 1870 federal census lists the couple as living with Louisa's father, a retired physician. Benjamin is listed as an invalid. He died on November 22, 1870, 55 years old.

33

Thomas Lloyd Vermeule

Thomas was born in Bridgeport New Jersey on June 11, 1814, the eldest of five children to the prominent physician, Dr. Richard Vermeule. The New Jersey Historical Society has extensive information on this colonial family. By 1820, the family was living in New York City where Thomas was educated as a lawyer.

A letter dated July 10, 1957, from the New York State Board of Law Examiners confirms they have no record of Thomas being admitted to the Bar to practice law. In 1846, he enlisted in the New York Volunteers and was appointed lieutenant in Company E. Soon after arriving in California, something else caught his attention:

> Things look still more gloomy this morning. We fear many more desertions will take place—Mr. Vermeule was arrested last night—We think he has been tampering with the men. His object has been to injure the Regiment all he could and raise a party for the gold mines—These mines will be the ruin of the Country as thousands of men are at work there now nearly in a state of starvation.

It's believed Thomas did complete his enlistment. His attempts at gold mining were not successful. He left the gold fields and settled in Stockton where he practiced law and wrote for a newspaper.

Fellow delegate and neighboring New Yorker Benjamin Lippincott, in describing the Convention to his sister, wrote, "T. Lloyd Vermeule sits alongside me and I can assure you no disgrace to our representation."

September 24. On motion of Mr. Wozencraft, Mr. Vermule, a member elect from San Joaquin, was introduced, sworn, and admitted to his seat.

September 26. Mr. Vermeule. I believe in abstract principles. I believe in their justice. If a principle be good in the abstract it must be good in practice; and I believe the right of appeal is a righteous abstract principle.

Mr. Vermeule. I am perfectly satisfied with the gentleman's explanation. Lawyers are a very useful body of men, and when this Constitution goes forth to the world it will be greatly indebted to them for the part they took in its formation.

October 3. Mr. Vermeule. I think, by the action of the House, we rather reserve the right to the people than deny them that right. I do not, for myself, know the views of the people who sent me here, upon this subject. I think it far better to leave the exercise of that right to them, than make it imperative upon the Legislature, at its first session, to pass this law.

In November 1849, Thomas was elected state senator but

The Delegates of 1849

resigned on April 10, 1850, to become city attorney for San Jose. He was also active in the California Democratic Party.

June 23, 1853. (Democratic State Convention) The minority also made a report reversing this order ... It was moved that the minority report be accepted, where on a very exciting and angry debate sprung up, Messieurs Broderick and Vermeule having some hard sparring. The former ... believe[d] there was something wrong, some trickery was designed and he was opposed to it. (Thomas was a staunch supporter of David Broderick.)

August 1853. When the name of Yontz was mentioned, Mister Vermeule arose and inquired if Mister Yontz would abide the decision of this convention. Mister Yontz in reply said that he belonged to the great Democratic Party and that he would abide the decision of that party. ... The cries of "We want no Bigler party man" were heard from various parts of the house –... At this stage Mister Vermeule arose and attempted to address the convention, bearing down pretty hard upon John Bigler and his clique. This aroused the Bigler portion of the convention who would not let him speak. ... [Soon] Vermeule and Yontz were both up on their feet trying to explain their positions; it was impossible to hear what they were saying for the confusion that prevailed.

On May 7, 1856, 42-year-old Thomas died as a patient at the Stockton Insane Asylum. The California State Archives does not have the Patient Index records for the period Thomas was there. All that is known is "Vermeule... was a bright man, but became insane ..."

34

Oliver Meredith Wozencraft

Oliver was born on June 26, 1814, in Clermont County Ohio to a father who emigrated from Wales and a mother from England. He was the youngest of five children and 11 years old when his father died. He left the family farm when he was 17 years old and began a life that would take him through several towns and as many adventures. He enrolled in St. Joseph's Jesuit College in Bardstown Kentucky and following graduation moved to Nashville Tennessee.

In February 1837, 22-year-old Oliver married 18-year-old Lemiza Ramsey. The couple would have six children, the first born in May 1838. They moved to Kentucky where he attended Louisville Medical College for three years.

Dr. Wozencraft set up his medical practice in New Orleans and became known for using quinine to cure yellow fever.

When the cholera epidemic broke out, he was asked to take charge of treating the indigent. His own health suffered as a result. The story goes that he traveled all the way to Brownsville Texas

(700 miles by land) to rest, and that is where he heard about gold being discovered in California.

He joined a small group of men heading for the California gold fields, taking the northwest route through Mexico and Arizona. After crossing the Colorado River, they wandered into the desert—their provisions depleted—and got lost. Two men died, Oliver collapsed. A younger and stronger man went in search of water. Was it while waiting in the hot desert for his traveling companion's return that a delirious Oliver conceived his wildest scheme—to irrigate the desert and transform it into farmland? Perhaps a mirage or two beckoned him.

Evidently, his gold mining did not pan out. He was back to practicing medicine in Stockton when he heard about the Constitutional Convention and was elected a delegate.

September 3. Mr. Wozencraft entered into an elaborate defense of the grounds upon which he claimed a seat in this Convention. He had been urged by his friends, much against his will, to submit his name as a candidate. It was known to many present that he had received a large vote in the district of San Joaquin, there being no opposing candidate. He came here knowing he had received this vote, and without the slightest expectation of being refused a seat. He had subjected himself to a great sacrifice of time and money in the hope of being enabled to serve that constituency who had conferred the honor of election upon him.

September 11 ... I desire to protect the people of California against all monopolies — to encourage labor and protect the laboring class. [He considered slavery a monopoly.]

September 12. [Wozencraft] supposed the majority of the members on this floor were not willing to deprive the descendants of Indians of the elective franchise. Many of the most distinguished officers of the Mexican Government are Indians by descent. At the same time, it would be impolitic to permit the full-blooded Indians who held property to vote. Those who held property, would, of course, be taxed. Capitalists could, for special purposes, make them purchasers of property. He was, therefore, in favor of the amendment as first proposed — to exclude all Indians. (Yet, protecting the Indian would be his next undertaking.)

Motivated by a fear of possible Indian uprisings, Congress on September 30, 1850, passed an act appropriating $25,000 for making peace treaties with the Indians of California.

Oliver was one of three men appointed as Indian commissioners. Their mission was to obtain information concerning Indian tribes residing within the boundaries of California: their manners, habits, customs, and extent of civilization, and to make such treaties and compacts with them as may seem just and proper.

The commissioners were doomed from the beginning. While they were given a great deal of responsibility in carrying out their mission, their instructions were vague, and they had no real support in Washington.

Oliver was convinced the Indians were being mistreated. Between May and September 30, 1851, he visited all the accessible tribes within his assigned region and negotiated with 81 bands, all under separate organizations and speaking about 12 different languages. He negotiated six treaties. He also suffered at least three attacks of fever.

On May 28, 1852, President Fillmore sent 18 treaties to the Senate. On June 28, 1852, they were all rejected. Unaware that they would need Congressional approval, several reservations had already been set up, and Indians placed on them. The Indians were never informed of the rejected treaties. The documents were made confidential to the Senate; and the secrecy was not revealed until January 18, 1905—53 years later.

The Indians carried out all of their agreements. The United States government took the land the Indians had agreed to surrender in the treaties and sold it as part of the public domain.

(On June 18, 2019, California Governor Gavin Newsom formally apologized to all California Native Americans through an executive order for the state's "dark history" of violence against indigenous people. "We can never undo the wrongs inflicted on the peoples who have lived on this land that we now call California since time immemorial, but we can work together to build bridges, tell the truth about our past and begin to heal deep wounds," Newsom said.)

Whether seen as a dream-chaser or a visionary, Oliver persevered.

November 1854 The project of establishing a stage route from Sacramento to Independence Missouri has of late attracted much public attention. ... Among its most conspicuous advocates stands Dr. Wozencraft who has published a series of instructive letters upon the question. ... Dr. W. is fully confident that the enterprise, besides its vast advantages to the State of California and to the nation at large would prove one of great profit to those who may invest ...

(Four years later, businessman and financier John Butterfield started the Butterfield Overland Mail Stage between St. Louis and San Francisco. It revolutionized mail and passenger service. Oliver did not benefit from this enterprise.)

The federal censuses of 1860, 1870 and 1880 listed Oliver, his wife and their children living in San Bernardino. He reported his occupation as a physician. While his attempts to improve the lives of the California Indians had a bitter outcome and the politics of the time hindered his efforts at establishing a stagecoach line, he never gave up on the pursuit of his dream to convert the Colorado River desert lands into fertile farmland.

> February 1877 Colorado Desert Lands. The House Public Lands Committee today had under consideration a bill to grant the lands known as the Colorado River desert to O.M. Wozencraft on condition of his reclaiming them by irrigation and furnishing a sufficient supply of water for the purpose of travel, etc. ... Wozencraft has arrived here to urge the passage of this measure and has brought to the attention of the Committee a favorable report ... by the House Public Lands Committee; also some extracts from reports of the Pacific Railroad surveys which assert its practicability. ...
>
> A report now being printed will show that the proposed diversion of the Colorado River cannot be successfully made at any point within the territory of the United States. The reasons for this conclusion of the Army Engineers are that the total amount of water which can be brought from the river at high water stages into the depressed desert would be inadequate to form a permanent lake of sufficient magnitude to noticeably change the climate by evaporation from its surface and that the small results attainable did not justify the necessary expenditure of money.

On November 22, 1887, 73-year-old Oliver died of a heart attack in a boardinghouse in Washington, D.C. where he had been attempting to present a Colorado Desert irrigation scheme bill to Congress intermittently for 14 years. Days before his death, the bill had been killed in committee.

Thirteen years after Oliver's death, work would begin on the Alamo Canal, ultimately providing irrigation to the Imperial Valley in a design similar to the one Oliver proposed nearly 50 years earlier. Thousands of acres of prime farmland have transformed the desert into one of the most productive farming regions in California with annual crop production in the early 21st century of over $1 billion dollars.

PART VII

San Jose District

35

Antonio Maria Pico

Antonio was born on January 1, 1808, in Monterey where his father, Sargent José Dolores Pico, was stationed in the Mexican Army. Sargent Pico was six years old when he accompanied his parents from Mexico on the second Anza Expedition to colonize Alta California. Antonio was the fourth of his parents' seven children who would survive beyond early childhood.

In November 1831, 23-year-old Antonio married 19-year-old Maria Pilar Bernal. They would become the parents of 12 children.

While Alta California was under Mexican rule, Antonio was alcalde of San Jose for several terms, a member of the territorial legislature and a colonel in the Mexican Army. Under the United States government, he also enjoyed an active and well-respected career.

He was at Colton Hall on the first day of the Constitutional Convention and remained to the last. He also joined the California Republican Party and was selected as a candidate for the presidential elector at the State Convention when Abraham Lincoln was nominated for the presidency.

April 1861 A Native Californian to Represent Us Abroad. Mr. Latham has advised the President to appoint some native Californian to represent the United States in some of the Spanish-American republics. The suggestion is an excellent one and deserves attention. ... Don Pablo de la Guerra undoubtedly has more experience in public affairs and is more familiar with the English language, but he is a zealous Democrat. ... Among the Republican natives is Antonio Maria Pico. ... [He] is more of a politician than any of the others, ... generally popular among both the American and the Spanish Californians. ... Some question, however, whether he has sufficient knowledge of law and the English language to represent us abroad, ... If he has that knowledge, there is no better man.

Mr. Pico is a reserved and modest, dignified gentlemen, and as such is not properly appreciated except by those who know him intimately. He has served in many positions of trust and honor requiring the exercise of more than ordinary ability, and is given satisfaction in all. In 1835, Antonio Maria Pico was alcalde of the Pueblo San Jose; Alcalde again in 1840; treasurer in 1842; Alcalde again in 1844, and at the same time the captain of the cavalry. In 1845, while still Alcalde, was appointed commander of the military which position he retained to the close of the war between United States and Mexico when he resigned his command and expressed his cordial allegiance to the United States government, when he was one of the first of the native Californians to perceive would give stability to the political affairs and speedy advancement in the material prosperity of his native country.

His character as a man of integrity and perfect uprightness and all the relations of social and business life, is above reproach. It appears therefore that there is but one requisite wanting—knowledge of the English language, and this difficulty it seems to me may be easily obviated by the employment of a secretary who possesses the necessary qualifications.

On May 28, 1869, 61-year-old Antonio died of inflammation of the lungs at his residence in San Jose.

36

Joseph Aram

Joseph was devoted to the land and would travel as far as was necessary to live on good soil. He was born on March 24, 1810, in Hartford New York, the eldest of ten children, all who grew up working on their father's farm. In 1835, 25-year-old Joseph married 22-year-old Mahala Birdsall who would die about a year later, leaving the widower with an infant daughter.

In 1838, Joseph married 25-year-old Sarah Ann Wright and resumed living the quiet life of a Hartford farmer, adding four children to the family. After seven years of working the land, Joseph was still dissatisfied with the yield. He heard there were better farming conditions in Illinois. He uprooted his family and took them nearly 1,000 miles west to Jo Daviess County.

After four years of farming, he realized he'd made a mistake. Illinois farming conditions were no better. The soil produced ague and malarial disease, and Joseph's health was failing.

News from California talked about very good farming conditions. Once again, Joseph packed up his wife and children, this time joining 11 other families heading overland for the Santa

Clara Valley. They started west in April 1846, the same month the Mexican-American War came to California.

Seven months and 2,000 miles later, the wagon train arrived at Sutter's Fort where it was welcomed by Captain Smith of Fremont's California Battalion. Smith had been detailed as a quasi-recruiting officer, first welcoming the weary immigrants, then persuading all the able-bodied men to postpone their settling and volunteer to fight for their new home in Fremont's Battalion.

Believing it was his patriotic duty, Joseph immediately enlisted and was appointed as captain. With a company of 31 men at his command, they escorted the immigrant families to Santa Clara where he made his headquarters. Hearing that a large force of mounted Mexicans was on its way to the Santa Clara Mission, he ordered his men to set up defenses and placed barricades across all the approaches.

Sounds of artillery and musket fire could be heard in the distance. Instead of joining the conflict, Joseph chose to keep his men at the Mission, protecting the women and children. Many of those women and children were the families of the soldiers out fighting.

Later, Joseph went to Monterey to help build a fort, then assisted in furnishing supplies to the troops and the Navy. It wasn't until 1849, three years after he had come to California, that he was free to begin his farming.

Joseph's patriotic duty extended to the Constitutional Convention. He was one of ten delegates who appeared in Colton Hall on the first day. During the third week, he was appointed to the committee on finance. He spoke only once during the Convention:

September 26. Mr. Aram. I think that this Convention should decide on some point as the permanent location for the seat of Government. Judging from the past, we have illustrations enough to satisfy us of the great importance of locating permanently at some central point.

San Jose is the geographical center of this State; it has none of the objectionable features of a commercial town. Being further inland than San Francisco or Monterey, it possesses the additional advantage of greater security in case of invasion. ... San Jose is central and salubrious—accessible from all parts of the country; and within a very short time there will be small steamboats plying to the Embarcadero, which is within six miles of the town. Maps of the plan of the town have not been exhibited here for show—it is a reality. And let me tell you that Washington Square is now composed of some sixty lots that would sell for a thousand dollars apiece. I feel perfectly confident that San Jose will eventually be the capital; and I am willing to let the matter rest with the people, for I believe they will be nearly unanimous in favor of that point.

After the Constitutional Convention, Joseph returned to the Santa Clara Valley and spent the rest of his life living in or near San Jose, eventually cultivating 40 acres of trees that became the first nursery in Santa Clara County. He served on the City Council for several years and was a trustee of the San Jose Academy as was fellow delegate Jacob Hoppe.

> September 8, 1851. The Trustees of the San Jose Academy desire to inform the public, that the English and Classical School which has been in operation in this city the last nine months, under the care of Rev. E. Bannister A.M., is to be enlarged and rendered permanent under the above appellation. For this purpose, the institution has been purchased and fitted for use, and the requisite arrangements

are being made to afford all the advantages desirable in a Boarding and Day School.

In 1873, Joseph's second wife Sarah died at the age of 60. Three years later, 66-year-old Joseph married the 42-old widow, Grace Devendorf. Joseph died on March 10, 1898, in San Jose. He was 88 years old.

In 1967, the City of San Jose donated a camellia bush that had outgrown its original space. Planted by Joseph in 1865, the 98-year old "bush" was 16 feet tall and 22 feet across, weighing between 13-15 tons and bearing approximately 5,000 blooms annually.

37

(Willard) Julian Hanks

Julian was born on Aug 3, 1810, in Tolland Connecticut, the fourth of eight children, and the sixth generation of his family to live in America since 1674. Julian left home for the sea at a young age, eventually becoming sea captain of a trading ship. Isabela Montana was born in Baja California. She was 14 years old in 1839 when she and Julian became parents to their first child and 32 in 1857 when their ninth and last known child was born.

Julian came to California in the mid-1840s and settled on a ranch near the Pueblo de San Jose where he was active in the new town's development. The following meticulous code, which bears no date except "1847," was signed by William Fisher, Chairman, James W. Weekes, Charles White, Antonio Sunol, Julian Hanks, Saber M. Castro, Isaac Branham, José Fernandez, and José Noriega.

WHEREAS, it is deemed essential to the interests of this pueblo, that a committee of twelve men be chosen from the inhabitants of the pueblo in respect to the building of bridges, regulating Acequia, and providing for and regulating the prisoners, who may from time to time be held for misdemeanors, therefore,

Resolved, that twelve men be elected to govern the pueblo and after they shall have been elected all their actions when in session shall be legal, ...

Resolved, that the following persons shall be constituted a committee for the better regulation of the pueblo, to wit: ... Captain Hanks, ... whose names were put before the Assembly and unanimously adopted and empowered to manage all things that might be beneficial to the interests of the pueblo at large.

The first duty of these newly created officers was the framing of a set Regulations for the better government of the Pueblo de San Jose de Guadalupe. The Articles are handed down to us in the following order:

    I. Be it ordained by this Council that it is requisite that the Pueblo St. Joseph be laid off into lots, blocks, squares and streets.

    II. Be it ordained that the main streets of this Pueblo be eighty feet wide and all the cross streets sixty feet wide.

    III. Be it ordained that there shall be two squares in this Pueblo, first Market square, and second, the Public square.

    IV. Be it ordained that the blocks shall contain one hundred yards square, and that the lots shall contain each fifty yards in front and fifty yards in depth unless that they are fractional.

    V. Be it ordained that the price of those lots shall be, each lot of fifty yards square, twelve dollars and fifty cents.

    VI. Be it ordained that one person may obtain four lots, or one block, and no more.

    VII. Be it ordained that those lots purchased by each individual shall be fenced, or a house erected thereon, on or before the expiration of twelve months from the date of purchase, otherwise to fall back to the Pueblo to the loss of the purchaser.

VIII. Be it further ordained that no house or edifice shall hereafter be erected with a cover of straw, grass, or flags, and all houses covered with said materials shall not be repaired after this date with the aforesaid materials. We further ordain that these shall be the laws of this Pueblo from this date until otherwise ordained.

In 1848, the first graveyard in Pueblo de San Jose was surveyed and laid out as 25 acres for Protestants and Catholics, and four acres for a Potter's Field. The first recorded burial took place on Nov 22, 1849—a child of Captain Julian Hanks. The child's wooden marker has long since weathered and disintegrated.

Julian arrived at Colton Hall for the Constitutional Convention on the afternoon of September 17 when he came forward, took the oath, and was admitted to his seat. He remained until the end, voting but never speaking.

During San Jose's charter election of April 1850, Julian was elected councilman.

In September 1867, Julian and his wife Isabela died. He was 57 years old and she was 42. No further information was available.

38

Kimball Hale Dimmick

Kimball was born on August 5, 1812, in Plymouth New York, into a family who came to America before 1639. He was the second of five surviving children, growing up on his father's small farm. As a young man, his dreams for his future did not include working the land. In 1831, he enrolled in Hamilton Academy in New York, supporting himself by teaching school in the winter, and working in a printing office.

In 1837, he joined the 105th Regiment of Infantry and was appointed quartermaster. In 1839, he began to study law in the office of Charles A. Thorp, Esquire and was granted his license three years later. He could now practice as an attorney in the New York State Supreme Court and act as a solicitor in the Court of Chancery of the State of New York. After taking all the exams to practice law—and passing them—he opened his law office in Norwich.

The following year he resigned from the 105th Regiment with the rank of brigadier general of the 32nd Brigade of Infantry. Seven months later, 31-year-old Kimball married 21-year-old

Sarah Holcomb. Having accomplished so much, his future success should have been assured; but that was not the case.

Less than three years later, in July 1846, Kimball enlisted in Stevenson's New York Volunteers and was appointed the captain of Company K, headed for California. "Necessity compels me to go. I have no other means of support." He left behind a wife, children, and considerable debt.

(What's unusual about Kimball joining Stevenson's Regiment is that Secretary of War, William L. Marcy, directed Stevenson that the regiment should be composed of "unmarried men, ... and such as would be likely to remain in California or adjoining territory at the close of the war.")

Kimball's leadership skills were put to the test from the start. After his men received their pay, they were told they had to buy their own uniforms, the ones they were wearing. His company unanimously refused. "The Regiment is on the point of breaking up. ... I do not think I shall ever go to California under Colonel Stevenson. The Regiment is in a perfect state of mutiny. Guards are posted, and no man can leave the island."

When Colonel Stevenson ordered the men to pay for their uniforms or take them off, Kimball's men took them off. He submitted his resignation, which was refused. In the meantime, his men made their own uniforms.

Kimball was a prolific letter-writer. After only one week, he wrote to his wife to "have courage and confidence in my return." He assured her he would return in about 18 months. But, as that time approached, he pushed his return date farther and farther ahead, saying first he would remain in the Army a few months longer, then until the war is over, then until the spring.

In August 1848, after being honorably discharged, he wrote to her that he would remain a few months, "but if I find I cannot make it profitable shall return home the first opportunity." He did make it profitable, and by January 1849, he had $20,000 in lots in the Pueblo de San Jose.

On April 25, 1849, he wrote that he would surely be home by spring. Yet, a letter written one week later contained a different sentiment. For the first time, he wrote "I should be happy to have you here." They'd been married only three years when he left for California and had been maintaining a long-distant relationship for another three years. She did not come.

On the first day of the Constitutional Convention, Mr. Kimball H. Dimmick, Esquire was appointed chairman pro tempore on a motion by Mr. Halleck. Kimball's remarks throughout the Convention proceedings stand out as being those of a mature and objective man who was very familiar with the law.

September 5. Mr. Dimmick wished to say a word before the question was put. He represented a portion of the California population in this House. The idea was prevalent that the native Californians were opposed to a State Government. This he did not conceive to be the case. He was satisfied from the conversations he had had with them, that they were nearly unanimous in favor of a State Government. As to the line of distinction attempted to be drawn between native Californians and Americans, he knew no such distinction himself; his constituents knew none. They all claimed to be Americans. They would not consent to be placed in a minority. They classed themselves with Americans, and were entitled to be considered in the majority. No matter from what nation they came, he trusted that hereafter they would be classed with the American people. The Constitution was to be formed for their benefit as well as to that of the native born Americans. They all had one common interest at stake, and one common object in view: the protection of government.

September 20. Mr. Dimmick. I trust, sir, that this amendment will not be adopted; for it certainly does appear to me to operate hard upon portions of the people of California. There are persons in this territory whom I consider justly entitled to be elected to the highest offices within the gift of the people, which this amendment would exclude. I mean the native Californians, whom I consider equally as well entitled to hold office as the American population. If it can be so modified as to include only those who become naturalized under the naturalization laws, I have no objection to the amendment; but when I see a proposition brought forward that will cut off the native-born citizens of California, I hope it will not be the pleasure of the Convention to adopt it.

September 25. Mr. Dimmick believed that a majority of the members were ready to vote upon all questions that might come up hereafter. He trusted the resolution would be adopted; and that gentlemen would shape their debates accordingly. For one, he was anxious to get through the business and go home; and he believed the majority of the delegates shared the same anxiety. The most important question to be decided was the judiciary system. This would not require debate; it would only be necessary to consider it calmly and deliberately, and then vote upon it.

October 2. Mr. Dimmick. I allude to no particular person. My remarks have reference to more than one. I was speaking of the uselessness of our spending the time of the people here upon questions which do not legitimately belong to us. Our decision can have no legal bearing upon this matter. We have already spent a great deal of time unnecessarily in debating questions of order. Most of the members are anxious to finish the business of the Convention and return to their homes. I trust that this resolution, and all other subjects foreign to our business, will be laid upon the table.

October 8. Mr. Dimmick wished to know whether this was a deliberative body sitting here to form a Constitution, or a mere debating society. This sort of discussion was children's play; it was a useless expenditure of the people's money. What was the object of this Convention? What were the members doing? He appealed to them to trifle away their time no longer; he trusted they would turn to their work in earnest, and confine themselves to the business before the House.

Near the close of the Constitutional Convention, Governor Riley appointed Kimball judge of the Supreme Court, likely at the recommendation of Henry Halleck. He proudly accepted the appointment and served until after the organization of the state government. His last official act was to administer the Oath of Office to California's first governor, Peter Burnett, at his inauguration.

In November 1850, Kimball did return home. His daughter had died while he was in California and another child would be born.

One year later, Kimball returned to California but no family came with him.

Had he come to sell his investments and return home with the money? Horrified, he discovered that in his absence he'd "been swindled, robbed of a fortune." He was broke.

He took a job at a printing office and wrote to his wife that he would try for a year to regain what he had lost, and again pleaded for her to join him. "If we were free from debt and you were only here with me … I might once more be happy." Again, she refused.

In January 1855, Kimball was appointed Los Angeles County judge. He died suddenly on September 11, 1861, of disease of the heart at the age of 49. He had recently been appointed United States district attorney for the Southern District of California. The six lots he had acquired in Los Angeles were sold at a probate sale.

39

Elam Brown

Elam was born on June 10, 1797, in Herkimer County New York. His Scottish parents moved to Ohio in search of fertile farmland soon after he was born. Elam was 18 years old when his father died. As the eldest son, with one brother and four sisters, he inherited the responsibility for maintaining the family farm.

When he was 21, Elam left home in search of his own fertile farmland, exploring through Missouri and Illinois. He eventually settled in Morgan County Illinois. Four years later, Elam married 21-year-old Sarah Allen and served as justice of the peace for 12 years.

In the fall of 1836, he relocated his wife and four children to the newly designated Platte Purchase bordering on the Missouri River where he cleared a farm of 180 acres. Sarah died in January 1843 when she was 41 years old. Three years later, Elam decided to move to the Pacific Coast and convinced several of his neighbors to join him. On May 1, 1846, with the widow Elam as captain, 14 families crossed the Missouri River at St. Joseph and headed west.

Assisting Elam in the captain duties was Isaac Allen, traveling with his wife Margaret and their 11 children.

The constant dangers of overland travel took their toll on the families of the wagon train. Several people came down with "plains fever," later discovered to be caused by drinking cow's milk, tainted from the animals eating poisonous brush. Some people died, including co-captain Isaac Allen.

Elam's wagon train reached Sutter's Fort on August 10, 1846. A few months later Elam agreed to join Fremont's California Battalion under the command of fellow-immigrant, Captain Joseph Aram and traveled to the Santa Clara Mission. There, in 1847, 50-year-old Elam married 53-year-old Margaret Allen, widow of co-Captain Isaac Allen.

The following spring, Elam hired out in the Contra Costa logging district. He helped to harvest trees, whip-sawed into lumber, haul the lumber by ox team to the Oakland Estuary, and transport it across the bay to San Francisco.

During one such delivery, Elam heard that the 3,300-acre Acalanes Rancho with 300 head of cattle was for sale. He had little money of his own, but his new wife had $900 she brought from Missouri, hidden in a clock. William Leidesdorff, the landowner, accepted Brown's $900 offer. Elam's first permanent home was a pre-cut frame house, erected two miles north of Lafayette. The new settlement was started.

Elam's remarks during the Constitutional Convention were phrased plainly and simply, easy for everyone, including interpreters, to understand.

September 13. Mr. Brown believed he would be in the minority on this question. It was a subject upon which he was very decided. Not only did he consider the question of economy involved in this case, but a question of much higher importance — public interest. Annual meetings of the Legislature would, in his opinion, be most injudicious as well as most expensive. If the Legislature passed laws every twelve months, those laws would have to go before the people. They would probably be in operation but six months when a new code of laws would be established. Sufficient time should be given to test all legislative enactments. He was convinced that the sudden changing of laws is a source of great public inconvenience, and is always attended by serious loss to individuals.

Mr. Brown. I am of opinion that it would be impolitic to place this clause in the Constitution. It may be susceptible of evil. The natural course of a representative is to obey the will of his constituents. He knows what they desire but if this provision is introduced in the Constitution, he may receive a letter with perhaps twenty or thirty names attached to it, instructing him to take a particular course. He has no instructions from the mass of his constituents; nevertheless, he knows that they entertain a different feeling — then the great majority of them do not wish him to take that course. But by this provision he is compelled to obey the wishes of twenty or thirty, and to disregard the will of perhaps several hundred.

September 26. Mr. Brown. I do not wish to be understood in that way. Perhaps my mode of expressing myself is not as distinct as it might be. There is an interest, a general interest in the decision of this question; and whenever we take an interest in any question, I think our views are apt to be tinctured in some degree by our profession or employment. I hope I shall not be considered as impugning the motives of any individual or class, by advancing this principle. There are private interests which affect every man to some extent. I consider this a question which involves these interests. Those who have made the law their study, and who gain their living by it, have opinions influenced, no doubt unconsciously, by the interests of that profession. Others form different opinions based upon different considerations. The question is one of very great importance. The experience of fifty years has shown me that lawsuits are unprofitable to the litigants; they are usually attended with costs, loss of time, ill feeling, and many other evil results to both parties. It is well, therefore, in my opinion, to embrace such features in our judiciary system as will operate as a check upon litigation. I conceive that it is not to the benefit of the community that these decisions should be carried from court to court at their expense. The community must suffer for it in the end, for whatever retards or diminishes the productive industry of the people individually, must operate to their disadvantage as a body. I am opposed to the principle of holding out inducements for appeals in every petty case that may arise.

After the Constitutional Convention, Elam served as alcalde of Lafayette from December 1849 until California became a state. He was also assemblyman to California's first two legislatures but turned down an offer to run for the Senate in 1852, saying he wanted to return to his farm where he raised cattle and grain. At the 1859 County Fair, he won grand prizes for his livestock draft stallions and a bull calf.

It could probably be said that Elam had finally found his fertile farmland. He died at home on August 10, 1889, 92 years old, after having a "shock of paralysis" from which he never recovered.

His obituary described him as having "sterling integrity of character and unflinching adherence to his convictions ... And yet with all his firmness and courage, proved on many a perilous occasion, he was one of the gentlest of men. He was an admirable conversationalist, and retained the clearness and vigor of his mind undiminished almost to the very close of life."

40

Pierre Sainsevain

Pierre was born in Beguey, Aquitaine France on November 20, 1818. In 1839, his mother sent him to California to find her brother, Jean-Louis Vignes, then living in Los Angeles. Pierre had no trouble finding Jean's thriving estate, El Aliso, where he was soon helping with growing grapes and oranges—and making wine.

By 1840, Pierre, as California's first wine wholesaler, was traveling by ship to Santa Barbara, Monterey, and San Francisco, selling his uncle's famous wine and brandy. A carpenter by trade, the following year Pierre was managing his uncle's sawmill business near San Bernardino.

In 1843, Governor Micheltorena granted Pierre the nearly 6,000-acre Rancho Cañada del Rincon on the San Lorenzo River near Santa Cruz. Already fluent in Spanish, the new landowner became a naturalized Mexican citizen and adopted the name, Don Pedro.

Later that year, he built his own sawmill, and the following year he started a flour mill. In 1845, 27-year-old Don Pedro married

18-old Maria Antonia Paula Suñol. The couple would have three sons: two born in California and educated in Bordeaux France, the youngest born in Bordeaux.

In the summer of 1846, Don Pedro and fellow Frenchman, Charles Roussillon built a schooner on the beach at Santa Cruz. They sailed the *Antonita* to the Sandwich Islands to have a copper bottom installed.

In 1848, Don Pedro and Roussillon tried their luck at gold mining near Coloma on the Tuolumne River. Returning to Stockton, they opened a store that supplied goods to the miners. The Don Pedro Reservoir behind the Don Pedro Dam across the Tuolumne River in the Stanislaus National Forest takes its name from Don Pedro's Bar mining town.

Months before the Constitutional Convention, Don Pedro and Roussillon began construction on an enormous two-story adobe on Market Square in San Jose, intending to run it as a hotel. With talk of moving the state capital to San Jose, Don Pedro offered the building to the city as the ideal location for the first state legislature.

The State bought the building for $50,000 and issued bonds. The bonds brought only 40¢ on the dollar. Don Pedro and Roussillon collected the balance in a lawsuit against the city.

Don Pedro came late to the Constitutional Convention and left early, perhaps for the same reason.

September 25. Mr. Dimmick gave notice that Mr. Pedro Sansevane, a delegate elect from San Jose, was present, and being entitled to take his seat under the report of the Committee on Elections, he asked that Mr. Sansevane be sworn in and permitted to take his seat. Mr. Sansevane was accordingly sworn, and took his seat.

September 26. Don Pedro Sansevaine. ... San Jose is the geographical center between the northern and southern parts of the country. By reference to Disturnel's map of Oregon and California, you will find that it is four degrees and forty minutes north of San Diego, and four degrees and forty minutes south of the forty-second degree of north latitude, which throws it exactly in the center. ... Another consideration: we must suppose that the native Californians in the south will have their members in our legislative halls, and I think they would choose at once San Jose in preference to any other point, from the fact there are a number of native Californians there, and it would be more agreeable to them to be among their countrymen and relatives. I presume the mind of every member of this house is made up that it is the proper place. A moment's reflection will convince any gentleman who is in doubt that San Jose is the most eligible and advantageous point.

October 6. On motion, leave of absence was granted to Mr. Sansevaine, in consequence of sickness in his family. [It's unknown who was ill at the time.]

Don Pedro's uncle was doing so well with his vineyards that several members of the extended family relocated to Los Angeles. Don Pedro's brother, Jean-Louis, arrived in 1855. Two years later, the brothers had their own storefront in San Francisco, selling Sainsevain Brothers wine, with a wine cellar producing California's first sparkling wine, similar to champagne. Uncle's El Aliso estate was the leading wine producer, turning out 125,000 gallons of wine and brandy.

In 1859, Don Pedro sold his rancho and, in partnership with his brother, bought their uncle's El Aliso vineyard for $42,000. Don Pedro also bought the Rancho Cucamonga vineyard in 1860. The brothers introduced "new and better" varieties of grapes. Three years later, grasshoppers destroyed everything.

In 1861, with California wines being sold on the East Coast for the first time, another Sainsevain Brothers shop opened—this one on Broadway in New York.

Don Pedro and Jean-Louis decided to experiment with bubbly wine. Champagne, sparkling wine production is always volatile. The brothers used mission grapes that weren't acidic enough, then aged the champagne for only one year instead of the recommended five or six years. During the first year, one out of every five bottles exploded. The champagne experiment cost them $50,000 and was shut down.

Later, their uncle's adult children sued them, accusing Don Pedro and Jean-Louis of paying their father considerably less than the true value for his vineyard. The cousins won the lawsuit. Don Pedro and Jean-Louis dissolved their winemaking business and sold El Aliso in 1869. The County Sheriff had to auction off their possessions and remaining wine stock to cover their debts.

Don Pedro moved back to Santa Clara County and produced wine under the Menlo Park label. When his wife Paula died in 1882 at age 55, Pierre returned to Bordeaux France where he died in October 1904 at the age of 86.

41

Jacob Durant Hoppe

Jacob was born on March 13, 1815, in Frederick City Maryland, a first-generation American to a German-emigrant father. He was the youngest of nine children, four years old when his father died.

In 1838, 23-old Jacob married 16-year-old Lucy Ewell. They would become the parents of eight children. Their first child was born in Missouri in 1840 where they lived for six years while Jacob supported his family as a merchant.

In 1846, he brought his family overland to California, settling in San Jose. When gold was discovered, he spent a few months around the mines, likely as a merchant. Business was good. Returning to San Jose, he was appointed the first postmaster.

> March 1848. All persons desiring to send letters or papers to the United States will please forward the same to our [post] office, prior to the first day of April. Postage on letters is 50 cents, on newspapers 12 ½ cents, to be paid in advance. We have made arrangements with Jacob D. Hoppe to superintend the business of the California office, who is duly authorized to attend to the collection of debts and

every other matter connected with the general business of the establishment.

He also purchased the *Californian*, the territory's first newspaper (begun in Monterey by Walter Colton and future-delegate Robert Semple in 1846, moved to San Francisco in mid-1847). It was not a good time to buy into the newspaper business as the following editorial explains.

> May 24, 1848. To our readers: with this slip ceases for the present the publication of the *Californian* ... The reasons which have led to this step are many and cogent. We shall however only state a few of them, merely to satisfy those whose curiosity may be aroused ... and to show the expediency of the measure.
>
> The majority of our subscribers and many of our advertising patrons have closed their doors and places of business and left town, and we have received one order after another conveying the pleasant request that "the printer will please stop my paper ... as I am about to leave for Sacramento." We have also received information that very many of our subscribers in various parts of the country have left their usual places of abode and gone to the gold region, owing that this fever is not confined to San Francisco alone. We really do not believe that for the last ten days, anything in the shape of a newspaper has received five minutes' attention from any one of our citizens. This, it must be allowed, is decidedly discouraging.
>
> The whole country, from San Francisco to Los Angeles and from the seashore to the base of the Sierra Nevada resounds with the sordid cry of gold! Gold! GOLD!!!! while the field is left half planted, the house half built, and everything neglected but the manufacture of shovels and pickaxes, ... In consideration of the state of affairs, and the degeneracy of the taste for reading consequent upon the rush for gold, where the word is "every man for himself," little regard for his neighbor, it would be a useless expenditure of labor and material to continue longer the publication of our paper. Had we a large amount

of capital to expand in the interval of dull times… We should still continue to print and publish our paper whether it was read or not. At the time when we took charge of it, the receipts were not only amply sufficient for its own support, but allowed for a handsome profit.

The *Californian* however, may by no means be considered as extinct, though for a time discontinued. Whenever the people of California resume the use of their reading faculties, we shall be ready to serve them with a newspaper, according to the best of our abilities. After this date, and until the publication of the paper is resumed or other notice given, the public are informed that no business whatever will be transacted in the name of J.D. Hoppe & Company; those interested will govern themselves accordingly.

In October 1848, Jacob left the newspaper business, writing that "he would highly recommend the new firm, now the proprietors of the *Californian* printing office, … believing them to be … practical printers from the best newspapers of the states, eminently persevering and well-qualified to conduct and continue the publication of a newspaper in this growing country."

Continuing with his civic engagement, in December 1848, Jacob served on the committee to consider establishing a provisional government for San Jose. In June 1849, he formed a partnership in a general wholesale and retail mercantile business and was elected a delegate to the Constitutional Convention.

> September 13. Mr. Hoppe looked upon this as a very important question. He admitted the fact stated by his friend from San Francisco, (Mr. Price) that the State of California would probably receive from the privilege of lottery-drawing, three hundred thousand dollars annually; and he admitted that it was a very desirable acquisition of revenue. But there is another ques-

tion involved in the adoption of this section — a question of far greater importance than money. It concerns the well-being of society, and the permanent industrial interests of the State. The system is not only objectionable in itself, but it is peculiarly objectionable in this country, where the temptation to gamble is so great. The effects are most deeply felt by those who are least able to sustain them. It penetrates to the domestic circle; it destroys the happiness of families, and falls with a peculiar weight upon the widow and the orphan. He appealed to this House not to sanction a principle so fatal to the best interests of society, by striking out the section.

October 4. Mr. Hoppe. I think our object should be to provide a fund sufficient for the education of every child in California. In order to get that fund, and have it appropriated to its legitimate purpose, it is necessary that we should secure it by constitutional provision. If we, in this Constitution, said that the 500,000 acres of land set apart by the Congress of the United States for educational purposes, shall be given, or the interest arising therefrom, for the benefit of common schools, and then place it in the hands of the Legislature to use it for other purposes, I think we go entirely too far, and violate the trust reposed in us.

Jacob was quite active following the Constitutional Convention. In October 1851, he was president of the Guadalupe Mining Company and a trustee for the San Jose Academy. He also speculated in real estate, in particular, the new community of Alviso that was the boating and shipping port of San Jose, and the transportation hub for the Santa Clara Valley to the San Francisco Bay. Steamboats regularly traveled between San Francisco and Alviso.

In 1852, Jacob acquired the 2,200-acre Rancho Ulistac from its original Ohlone Indian grantees. Rancho Ulistac extended across lowlands reaching from the Alviso shoreline southward and encompassing the land between the Guadalupe River and Saratoga Creek. It was prime real estate with a profitable future.

> April 12, 1853. We are again called upon to record one of those awful catastrophes, incidental to steam navigation, ... Yesterday at about [12:30 PM], as the steamboat Jenny Lind was on her passage to this City [San Francisco] from Alviso, ... [the] boiler blew out. ... The terrible loss of life is owing to the fact that the major part of the passengers had just sat down to dinner, and were in a direct line with the boiler when the explosion occurred. If the explosion happened about five minutes previous, not a soul would have been injured as the cabin was empty.

Jacob was traveling on the *Jenny Lind* that day, about to enjoy his midday meal. He died five days later, on April 17, 1853. He was 38-years-old. His obituary described him as " ... an enterprising and public-spirited citizen, an earnest friend of California (representing her warmly in every enterprise in which he was engaged) and an esteemed friend and companion wherever his virtues were known."

PART VIII

San Luis Obispo District

42

Henry Amos Tefft

Henry was born on August 24, 1823, in Union Village New York, into a family whose American roots went back seven generations to 1638. He attended law school, then joined his parents and sisters in Wisconsin where, on August 10, 1848, he was appointed U.S. postmaster of Two Rivers, located on the shore of Lake Michigan.

In early 1849, Henry came down with gold fever and headed for California's gold country. He traveled overland to Santa Fe New Mexico and along the Gila River route to San Diego where he boarded a ship heading north to San Francisco. Near the central coast, a scene played out that would repeat a few years later—with tragic consequences.

Seasonal strong winds and rough seas had forced the ship to lay to at several places along the coast. When it dropped anchor inside the natural harbor of Port San Luis, Henry went ashore where it's said he fell in love with the beauty of the area and abandoned his plans of gold mining.

He traveled the seven hilly miles into San Luis Obispo and

found the former Mission community to his liking. He also met the hospitable Captain William Dana who offered him lodging, which is where Henry met his future wife. Four months later, Henry was on his way to Monterey to represent his adopted home as its delegate to the Constitutional Convention. He was present on the first day.

September 12. ... He hoped this question [of allowing Indians the privilege of voting] would be considered calmly and dispassionately in all its bearings, and that gentlemen would not, by acting hastily, exclude all Indians, ... from the right of suffrage. Had they considered well the feeling that would go abroad among the native population of California, if injustice was done to this class of people?

September 18. [Tefft] Now, I am willing to go as far as the gentleman from San Francisco, ... in prohibiting banks or the circulation of bank paper, but I cannot vote for the amendment making it a penal offence to pass a certificate of deposit. The question of currency is one of momentous import. It should never have been made a party question in the States—subject to the fluctuating influences of political factions. ... I am very sure, sir, that no member of this Convention can be blind to the disastrous results of the banking system, ...

September 22. Mr. Tefft. There are periods in the proceedings of every deliberative body, when calm investigation should follow the excitement of debate; and if that period is at any time arrived, I believe it is the present. I consider this question of the boundary decidedly the most important that has yet been debated. ... As delegates of this Convention, I consider it our first duty to inquire the situation in which we find California.

September 26. Mr. Tefft. I think if the gentleman from Monterey (Mr. Botts) would discriminate between the words charge and declare in the section, he would arrive at different conclusions. ... I do not desire that the judge should have power to charge juries, but that he may have the privilege of declaring to the jury the law and the facts. It would be a singular feature in this Constitution to declare that he should not have that power. Declaring the facts is a very different thing from the old system of charging the jury, or requiring the jury to find a certain verdict.

September 27. Mr. Tefft. It is not my intention, on this occasion, to enter into any discussion as regards the two systems of civil and common law; neither is it my intention to argue here upon the rights of women in general, and married women in particular; ... This is undoubtedly a matter of great importance. ... It was said this evening that this was an attempt to insert in our Constitution a provision of the civil law. Very well—suppose it is; there are gentlemen in this House wedded to the common law; I am myself greatly attached to it; but that does not prevent me from seeing many very excellent provisions in the civil law.

October 4. Mr. Tefft. Suicidal as the gentleman from Monterey (Mr. Botts) thinks this course, I think we will adopt it. I am as much in favor of referring all power to the people as any gentleman present, ... Let political excitement run wild here as it has in every State of the Union, then you will find the absolute necessity of the two-third rule. It is of essential importance, that in amending the fundamental law of the land men should return to their sober second thought—to that great balancing power by which questions so deeply concerning the interests of the whole people are decided.

October 10. Mr. Tefft. When the question was originally taken in this House whether we should form a State or Territorial organization, certain delegates voted in favor of a Territorial Government, but not in favor of having a Territorial Government south and a State Government north. ... From the excited state of feeling manifested in this House yesterday, I am opposed to bringing up this boundary question again, without the assurance that there is now a spirit of conciliation in the House. I am opposed to having tables knocked down as they were yesterday in this madness of excitement.

After the Constitutional Convention, Henry was elected to the first legislative assembly as the representative from San Luis Obispo County but resigned when offered the position of justice of the Second Judicial District.

After establishing his professional career, 26-year-old Henry married William Dana's eldest daughter, 21-year-old Maria Josefa on July 9, 1850. The traditional Mexican wedding, which lasted for several days, was the premier social event of the year.

By January 1852, Henry's life seemed to be unfolding in perfect order. He was a successful lawyer and judge, a member of a prominent California family, and Maria Josefa was pregnant with their first child. Yet, a letter from his parents pleading with him to come home caused Henry to suddenly give it all up to return to Racine Wisconsin.

He resigned his judgeship, closed his law practice, and sold all his property. He also confided to a friend that he had a premonition he would never see Racine; yet, he continued to prepare for their departure.

On February 6, 1852, having completed his business in Santa Barbara, Henry boarded the coastal steamer *Ohio* bound for San Francisco, with stops along the way. One of those stops was at Port San Luis where Henry wanted to bring his wife aboard. The weather conditions were similar to the ones that brought Henry to San Luis Obispo three years earlier: strong winds, high waves, and heavy surf.

When the *Ohio* neared Port San Luis, Henry would not listen to the captain's warnings that it was too dangerous to be in the water. The captain acquiesced and sent Henry with five sailors in a dinghy headed to shore. One hundred yards out, the boat capsized in surf strong enough to drown three able-bodied sailors—and 29-year-old Henry. His body was never recovered. Somehow, Maria Josefa's family kept the news of her husband's tragic death from her for some time. Henry Junior was born but did not survive infancy.

Despite his reputation for being cold and indifferent, Henry Halleck wrote a letter of condolence to William Dana, Henry's father-in-law. "Permit me, my dear sir, to offer to your family and to Mrs. Tefft, my deep sympathies in her bereavement; I knew [Henry] well, and had become attached to him by strong feelings of friendship and esteem and keenly regret his loss." Henry Halleck had offered his home to the young, hardworking delegate during his stay in Monterey.

43

José Maria Covarrubias

José's political philosophy was that it is the duty of every citizen to serve his country gratuitously when the circumstances require it. To his credit, his service to both the Mexican and U.S. governments provided stability in those uncertain times.

He was born on January 25, 1806, in Cadiz Spain, where his father was a merchant. He was the third of six children and quite young when his mother died.

By 1834, José was living in San Blas Mexico, having become a naturalized citizen. He was selected by the organizers of the Hijar-Padres Expedition to be one of the 239 Mexican citizens brought to California to strengthen the Mexican population against the growing influence of the United States and Russia. The colonists were offered free transportation, a per diem cash allowance, land, and a livestock provision when they arrived at the Pueblo de Monterey. José had hired on to be a teacher; but once in Alta California, he gave up the teaching position for a political career with the Mexican government.

In June 1838, 32-year-old José married 24-year-old Maria

Carrillo, the niece of future fellow-delegate, José Antonio Carrillo. They were parents to eight children.

In 1844, José served as alcalde of Santa Barbara and acting secretary of state for the Department of California under Governor Pio Pico.

In 1845, he and his brother-in-law, Joaquín Carrillo received a land grant to the 26,600-acre Rancho Castaic in Santa Ynéz Valley. It was said that they hired Native American laborers to work on his cattle ranch.

At the Constitutional Convention,
September 6. Resolved, That Messrs. P. La Guerra, and J. M. Covarrubias, now at the bar of this House, have produced to this House satisfactory evidence of having been duly elected members of this Convention from the districts of San Luis and Santa Barbara, and that they be requested to come forward and be qualified as such. Adopted.

September 28. The question recurring on Mr. Jones' resolution, Mr. Covarrubias moved the following amendment: Resolved, That it being the duty of every citizen to serve his country gratuitously when the circumstances require it, the delegates of this Convention shall receive no compensation whatever for their services.

The first legislative election was held one month after the Constitutional Convention. José was elected the state assemblyman for Santa Barbara. He was re-elected eight more times, serving through 1861 when he became a justice on the Santa Barbara County Court.

In 1850, José bought Santa Catalina Island for $10,000 from Thomas Robbins, who had received the island as a land grant from Governor Pio Pico. Three years later he sold it for an undisclosed amount.

In May 1853, José was appointed the surveyor of the Port of Santa Barbara.

José died on April 1, 1871, in Santa Barbara, 65 years old.

PART IX

Santa Barbara District

44

Pablo de la Guerra

When Pablo's father was a young boy in Novales Spain, he dreamed of being a war leader. In 1792, 13-year-old José de la Guerra was sent to Mexico City in Colonial Mexico, New Spain. The following year he joined the Frontier Army, and in 1815 was stationed at the Santa Barbara Presidio. In 1827, he was promoted to commandant, a position he would hold until 1842 when he retired after 52 years of loyal military service.

Pablo was born on November 29, 1819, in Santa Barbara, the fourth of eleven children. As a boy, he was sent away to be educated. When he returned, he served as the collector of customs for the Port of Monterey. In 1842, he was the administrator of the Monterey Custom House, a position he would hold for two years. Following the Bear Flag Revolt in 1846, Pablo refused to lower the Mexican flag at the Custom House.

In 1844, Governor Micheltorena granted the 56,600-acre Rancho Nicasio to Pablo and John Cooper, Thomas Larkin's half-brother.

In 1847, Pablo was appointed alcalde of Santa Barbara. On

March 12th of that year, 27-year-old Pablo married 17-year-old Josefa Moreno in the Chapel of the San Carlos Mission in Monterey. They became the parents of five children. Their firstborn son, José Antonio, would be educated at Georgetown, and the second, Juan, in England where he earned three degrees.

At the Constitutional Convention,

September 6. Resolved, that Messrs. P. La Guerra, and J. M. Covarrubias, now at the bar of this House, have produced to this House satisfactory evidence of having been duly elected members of this Convention from the districts of San Luis and Santa Barbara, and that they be requested to come forward and be qualified as such. Adopted.

September 12. Mr. [de la Guerra] desired that it should be perfectly understood in the first place, what is the true signification of the word "white." Many citizens of California have received from nature a very dark skin; nevertheless, there are among them men who have heretofore been allowed to vote, and not only that, but to hold the highest public offices. It would be very unjust to deprive them of the privilege of citizens merely because nature had not made them white.

September 29. Mr. [de la Guerra] said he could easily remove the fears entertained by the last speaker, that such an overflowing amount of Indians would vote. There was no such desire on the part of any member of that Convention, He did not at all desire that the mass of Indians should vote, and he had expressly said so. All the Indians in the entire Territory who owned land and were entitled to vote, under the laws of Mexico, were not more than two hundred; he was perfectly satisfied of it. For himself, he only proposed that those who were entitled to a vote by virtue of holding property, purchased under the Mexican laws prior to the cession of California, should still be permitted to exercise that right. There was no fear of two hundred votes having any serious effect in a population of 60,000.

Pablo's sister, doña Augusta Jimeno, lived in Monterey where her home was a favorite gathering place for Convention delegates, both American and Californio. Despite her bitter opposition to the American occupation, she was pleasant and congenial toward her American guests. When her husband, Don Manuel Jimeno, secretary of state under General Alvarado died, she married Dr. James Ord, brother of delegate Pacificus Ord.

In 1851, in direct violation of the 1848 Treaty of Guadalupe Hildago which provided that existing land grants would be honored, Congress passed the Land Law. It required all former Mexican citizens living in the "new" territories to provide proof of ownership of their land grants. This was nearly impossible, considering the lack of documentation. In the meantime, another law allowed Anglo Americans to seize and develop the land while the cases were being disputed. Pablo was the lone voice against this injustice. The following are excerpts from his remarks before the State Senate in April 1855:

> I hope the Senate will allow me to offer a few remarks upon the merits of the bill, and to state why, upon the principles of reason and justice I consider that the bill should be indefinitely postponed.
>
> Well, sir, the war took place, and we, after doing our duty as citizens of Mexico, were ... abandoned by our nation, and as it were, awoke from a dream, strangers on the very soil on which we were

native and to the manor born. We passed from the hands of Mexico to that of the United States, but we had the consolation of believing that the United States, as a nation, was more liberal than our own. ... a nation that was the most careful in protecting the just rights of its citizens.

I believe that I speak advisedly, when I say that three-fourths of the settlers upon the lands, have been aware that someone had a prior claim; they knew it by common report, ... but they thought that even if it was confirmed to the owners, that the use of the land until the confirmation, would be worth more than the improvements that they would make ...

Now, sir, of the one hundred, thirteen members in this Legislature, I am the only native of this state; and the native population expect from me, and through me, that in my place in this Legislative Hall, that I shall call the attention of this body to the facts I have now stated, and to tell you that badly treated as they have been in every respect, they look around them and find no other aid except ... the justice of this Legislature; and now, in their name, I call upon you, Senators, to consider that if they are deprived of what is left to them, they have no other place to go to. ... they, through me, throw themselves upon your mercy and clemency; and they ask and expect from you protection that will justify before the eyes of the world the belief in justice of the American people. ... And, sir, to conclude these remarks, permit me to assure you, upon my honor as a gentleman, that everything I have stated is true and as clear as conviction itself. I know that I am in the Senate Chamber of California, where full liberty of speech is allowed, but if I were speaking to a barbarous people, I should still advocate the same sentiments, and even if I were killed for so doing, I should at least have the satisfaction of dying in a just cause, ..."

Pablo succeeded in tabling one land seizure bill after another. A cascade of political pressure ultimately overwhelmed his cause, as

The Delegates of 1849

more white settlers and miners moved to California and demanded to "reclaim" the land.

In 1861, as leader of the State Senate, Pablo served as the acting lieutenant governor. In 1869, he ran for district judge. His opponents challenged his right to the office because Congress had failed to formally grant citizenship to Pablo and other Californios. He sued.

In the landmark case of People v. de la Guerra (1870), the California Supreme Court upheld Pablo's right to run for public office, arguing that when California was admitted as a state, former Mexican nationals automatically became citizens. He won the election and was still in office at the time of his death.

Pablo died on February 5, 1874, at the age of 55. He had suffered from asthma for a long time. Approximately 2,000 mourners attended his funeral.

45

Jacinto Rodriguez

Jacinto Rodriguez was born on January 12, 1815, in the Pajaro Valley, now the City of Watsonville. He was the third of twelve children, his Mexican ancestry tracing back six generations. Soon after his father's death, Jacinto moved to Monterey, where he held numerous positions within the Mexican government.

In 1847, Jacinto began construction on an adobe home in Monterey. He also started buying up the nearby property. Two years later, he would welcome fellow Constitutional Convention delegates into his home.

In July 1848, 33-year-old Jacinto married 19-year-old Maria Peregrina Pinto. They would become the parents of five children.

Although Jacinto lived in Monterey, he represented the Santa Barbara District at the Convention where he was appointed to the boundary committee.

Years after the Convention, Jacinto spoke with Mariano Vallejo who was in Monterey visiting his sister. "My dear General," he said. "Please forgive my attire, for since I finished my work at the Convention ... I have not paid much attention to my appearance, and you can understand this very well, for great men are aware of the sudden changes in fortune to which those who take part in framing constitutions are exposed. I assure you that if the people should call upon me another time for public duties, I would not serve again. I sacrificed myself once, but they will not get me a second time."

Jacinto died on Dec 14, 1878. He was 63 years old.

PART X

Sonoma District

46

Robert Baylor Semple

Robert was born on February 3, 1806, in Mt. Radiance Kentucky, the fifth of nine children to Scottish parents whose ancestors came to America in the early 1700s. His father died when Robert was 14 years old. His restless nature emerged at a young age.

Apprenticed to learn the printing trade, he didn't like it, then studied dentistry and didn't like it, either. He did, however, enjoy the study of medicine. After graduating from Transylvania University in 1825, he practiced successfully for many years in Kentucky. He married Sally Parrish, and their son was born in 1831. Ah, the content life of a country doctor, or was it?

While Lansford Hastings anticipated that his *Emigrant's Guide to Oregon and California* would inspire thousands of settlers to join him in 1845 on his next overland expedition, only 22 people signed up. Only half of them completed the perilous journey, Robert among them.

As to why Robert came to California, there's speculation that he was on a mission for the U.S. government. Fellow Kentuckian,

James Polk had recently been elected U.S. president. Robert's family was politically intimate with James and likely knew of his interest to acquire California from Mexico. Once in California, Robert had a knack of never being far away when an important event was unfolding.

On June 14, 1846, he was among the 33 rebels who carried out the Bear Flag Revolt. They reached Sonoma in the early morning hours and surrounded the home of General Mariano Vallejo, Mexican Commandant of Northern California. They arrested General Vallejo and imprisoned him at Sutter's Fort.

Two months later, Robert was in Monterey, assisting Walter Colton with publishing the first California newspaper.

> <u>August 15, 1846</u>. Today the first newspaper ever published in California made its appearance. … It is to be issued on every Saturday and is published by Semple and Colton. … My partner is an emigrant from Kentucky, who stands 6 foot 8 in his stockings. He is in a buckskin dress, a Fox skin cap; is true with his rifle, ready with his pen, and quick at the type case.
>
> [Robert] created the materials of our office out of the chaos of a small concern, which had been used by a Roman Catholic monk in printing a few sectarian tracks. … the mice had burrowed in the balls; there were no rules, no leads, and the types were rusty and all pi. It was only by scouring the letters could be made to show their faces. A sheet or two of tin were procured, and these, with a jack-knife, were cut into rules and leads. Luckily we found, with the press, the greater part of a keg of ink; and now came the main scratch for paper. None could be found, except what is used to envelop the tobacco of the cigar smoked here by the natives. … It is in sheets a little larger than the common sized foolscap. And this is the size of our first paper, which we have christened *The Californian*.
>
> … Our first number is … full of news. … We have received by couriers, during the week, intelligence from all the important mili-

tary posts through the territory. Very little of this has transpired; it reaches the public for the first time through our sheet. We have also, the declaration of war between the United States and Mexico, with an abstract of the debate in the Senate. The crowd was waiting when the first sheet was thrown from the press. It produced a quite a little sensation. ... When half of the paper is in English, the other in Spanish. W. COLTON

When Commodore Robert Stockton visited San Francisco the latter part of September 1846, Robert was there and managed to return to Monterey in style:

October 17, 1846. After an absence of some weeks on a tour of observation, for the purpose of establishing a mail, ... through the country, I am glad to sit again in my own chair. The object of my visit is in a good way of being accomplished. His Excellency, the Governor General is making arrangements for a regular transportation of the mail, and I hope, that in a few weeks, at most, we shall be able to deliver our papers and letters at all the principal points in the country. I am pleased to have it in my power to return my thanks to Commodore Stockton, for a very pleasant passage in the Congress, ... and years will pass away, before my mind will cease to revert with pleasure, to the time passed in company with the officers of the Congress. R. SEMPLE.

Following General Vallejo's release two months later, Robert was escorting him back to Sonoma when they passed the Strait of Carquinez. Robert immediately saw the potential of a thriving town, then Mariano told him he owned the land. The wheels started turning.

Before Robert returned to Monterey, a deal had been struck. Mariano would donate the land for a city to be named Francisca after his wife. Surveyors were immediately hired and began laying out lots and streets. Notices of the transaction were printed in the newspaper.

<u>December 22, 1846</u>. Mariano Vallejo ceded in favor of Robert Semple ... five miles of land on the estate of Soscol in the Straits of Carquinez ... with the object of founding in said land the city to be called Francisca.

<u>April 24, 1847</u>. Mariano Vallejo and Robert Semple, proprietors, advertise lots for sale in the City of Francisca with the intent of developing the city.

Meanwhile, across the bay in Yerba Buena, that city's developers became alarmed that the new town planned at the Strait of Carquinez would rival their own. Knowing the importance of a name, the City Council hastily voted to officially change the name of Yerba Buena to San Francisco. Robert was outraged. He, in turn, changed the name of his town to Señora Vallejo's middle name, Benicia. Legal notices regarding Benicia appeared regularly in local newspapers. Thomas Larkin entered the picture.

<u>May 19, 1847</u>. ... the partnership between Mariano Vallejo and Robert Semple is dissolved.

<u>May 19, 1847</u>. I, Mariano Vallejo, ... lawful owner of the estate known by the name Soscol ... do declare in my own name ... That I cede and transfer freely and spontaneously in favor of Don Thomas O. Larkin and Dr. Robert Semple.

On May 22, 1847, the *Californian* was relocated to San Francisco. While not mentioning Benicia by name, the reason for the move is quite apparent.

... The most important reason for our leaving Monterey was not that we disliked the place, or the people, for we were highly pleased with both; but we have been fortunate enough to secure a valuable landed interest on the Bay of San Francisco, on which we are laying out a town. ... We were anxious to be as near to our interest as possible; while we were satisfied that we could make the *Californian* equally, if not more useful to our patrons by publishing it at this place. ...

June 5, 1847. A plan of the city of Benicia may be seen at the office of the *Californian*. Persons wishing to purchase lots at private sale can now have an opportunity of doing so, by applying to R. Semple, Californian office.

June 30, 1847. (Publishes Articles of Agreement between Larkin and Semple, binding them as partners to develop Benicia.)

In July 1847, Robert resigned from the *Californian*, and B. R. Buckelew became the new owner/publisher. Robert then became a frequent advertiser in his former newspaper.

July 1847 Ferry at Benicia City. In establishing the rates of ferriage across the bay, I had referenced the gentle horses which might be led into the boat. But as wild horses and mares have to be tied and hauled in, I have been under the necessity of charging $.50 each more than for tame horses. I have now in progress a splendid horse boat which will be propelled by wheels with four horses and will be ready by the first of September. The boat will be secured for any kind of stock and the prices will then be regulated. R. SEMPLE

August 1847. New Store at Benicia City. The subscriber has just opened a small assortment of dry goods and groceries at the Benicia

City. He will sell at San Francisco prices, for prompt payment in cash or hides. R. SEMPLE

September 1847. New Ferry House at Benicia. The subscriber is now building a house on the opposite side of the Straits for the comfort and accommodation of persons wishing to pass from the south side. He intends hereafter to keep a boat on each side, that persons will not be detained a moment longer than the tide and weather requires. He has and will keep on hand, barley and corn for horse feed. R. SEMPLE

The first wedding to occur in Benicia was his own, on November 28, 1847. Forty-one-year-old Robert married 22-year-old Frances Cooper whose father had been a guide and scout with Fremont. (At the time, Robert was still married to Sallie Parish, still living in Kentucky, while their son, John, was living with Robert in Benicia. Sallie's divorce from Robert would not be final until February 28, 1849.)

By January 1848, 200 lots had been sold in Benicia City which received the first news of the discovery of gold at Sutter's Mill. The town quickly grew as a major hub for travel to all points, including sea-going vessels. It was a gala day for Benicia when Commodore Thomas Jones ordered the *Southampton* to proceed up the waters of the unchartered bay to Benicia, to make soundings for channels, inspect anchorages and view the new townsite.

The commodore eventually purchased 23 lots and two business blocks. Many of his officers also bought a property. Needless to say, the activity at Benicia was closely watched by the leading men of San Francisco who began a campaign to head off the rival. But, in the meantime:

The Delegates of 1849

<u>March 1848.</u> Ferry at Benicia City. Persons wishing to pass the Bay of San Francisco will hereafter find a good substantial ferryboat at the Straits of Carquinez. There is a good level road from the mission of Santa Clara Mission to San Jose distance 50 miles, from Benicia City to Sonoma 25 miles, from Benicia City to new Helvetica 50 miles. Rates of ferriage: for crossing a man and horse—$1. R. SEMPLE, proprietor

General William T. Sherman, then stationed in California, used Robert's Ferry and later wrote about it in his memoirs:

We found there a solitary adobe-house, occupied by Mr. Hastings and his family, embracing Dr. Semple, the proprietor of the ferry. This ferry was a ship's-boat, with a lateen-sail, which could carry across at one tide six or eight horses. ... It took us several days to cross over, and during that time we got well acquainted with the doctor, who was quite a character..... That Benicia has the best natural site for a commercial city, I am satisfied; and had half the money and half the labor since bestowed upon San Francisco been expended at Benicia, we should have at this day a city of palaces on the Carquinez Straits.

Robert was among the first 10 delegates to arrive at Colton Hall on September 1st, the official first day of the Constitutional Convention, having risen from his sick bed to attend. He had contracted typhoid fever which runs its course in about four weeks, leaving the patient exhausted and emaciated.

When Snyder accused Gwin of wanting to be president of the convention, Gwin leaped to his feet and could do no less than disclaim anything of the kind or that he brought a Constitution there for the purpose of having it adopted. Then Snyder said if that was the case he would nominate Doctor Semple as president of the convention and with a sort of laugh he was elected.

A hush fell upon the assemblage with the elongated frontiersman was escorted to his seat of honor by Mariano Vallejo and John Sutter. ... Many who were present remembered when Vallejo and Sutter were sovereigns of rival kingdoms. And few would forget that Vallejo had once been the prisoner of Semple and Sutter.

The records show that Robert was unable to preside at several Convention sessions because of illness, but he never resigned or was asked to step down. Not one to sit quietly on the sidelines, he occasionally appointed someone else to sit in for him as president so he could step down long enough to join the conversation.

September 13. Mr. Semple called the gentleman's attention to a system known as gerrymandering in the States, and explained the effects of that system. He was in favor of the section; he considered it a necessary provision in the Constitution to provide against political frauds of this kind, and if there never had been such a provision reported before, he thought the Committee would deserve credit for originating so excellent a provision.

September 24. Mr. Semple. I feel under some obligation to repeat a conversation which has a direct bearing upon this matter. There is a distinguished member of Congress ... now in California. With a desire to obtain all the information possible ... I asked him what was the desire of the people in Congress; I observed to him that it was not the desire of the people of California to take a larger boundary than the Sierra Nevada; and that we would prefer not embracing within our limits this desert waste to the east.

His reply was: "For God's sake leave us no territory to legislate upon in Congress." He went on to state then that the great object in our formation of a State Government was to avoid further legislation. ...

September 25. Mr. Semple. ... I propose here to put all the wealth of the rich townships into this general fund, so that the poor ones may get a share of it. In regard to the question of constitutionality, my own opinion is that there is no law enacted by Congress which prohibits the State of California from making a general school fund. ...

September 27. Mr. Semple. Dueling itself is, so far as I am individually concerned, unconstitutional. My constitution forbids it, and I have resolved never to fight a duel if I can honorably get out of it. ... I would dislike very much to fight a duel, because I might be killed. I consider that one of the strongest objections to the practice.

After the Constitutional Convention, while traveling north with fellow delegates, Robert pointed out several locations in the desolate mountain passes. He told his companions that was where he had hidden on his night rides as a messenger between San Francisco and Monterey during the Mexican-American War.

Feb 1851. It will be seen by our advertising columns that our friend General Semple, the original founder of Benicia, is determined not to be in the way of holding up his property... Thereby preventing the improvement of the straits. He offers 1000 lots at $50 each, to be determined by the drawing of a lottery... We have no doubt that the back lots are worth the money and those through the middle of the city and on the Bay said to be worth now from $1000 to $4000. Every holder of the ticket must get a lot as there are no blanks.

<u>Colusa May 22, 1852</u>. Today our quiet community was in an unusual state of excitement, consequence of the election .... On the closing of the polls, Dr. R. Semple... was declared elected justice of the peace. In the afternoon a meeting of the squatters took place... The object being to devise some plan by which titles to the land they had improved would be guaranteed them. The meeting was ably addressed by Dr. Semple, his brother Col. Semple and Mr. Pickett all of whom advocated employing competent lawyers to attend the squatter interests of the Board of Land Commissioners.

<u>July 1853</u>. Fire at Benicia. Wells Fargo & Company's messenger informs us that a fire occurred yesterday in the government buildings at Benicia to the amount of about $10,000. No other particulars.

Benicia became the state capital in 1853, and for a while, it looked like Robert's dreams for his town would come true. But the following year, when the legislature convened, and there were no accommodations for the 100 men, the delegates from Sacramento made an offer no one could refuse. When the railroad came to California, the harbor was no longer a major hub for travel. Even Robert left Benicia.

He purchased rich pasture lands on Freshwater Creek in Colusa County, naming his new home Almo Rancho. In the late summer of 1854, while riding his trusty little Mexican pony to Marysville, Robert came upon the cowboys who were moving his cattle to the new ranch. The cowboys offered Robert a fresh horse, which he accepted. It's believed the bigger horse did not like Robert's spurs and violently bucked him off. Severely injured, Robert was taken to Almo Rancho where he died a few days later on October 25, 1854, at the age of 48.

On December 6, 1957, at their first annual meeting, the California Press Association included Doctor Robert Baylor Semple among the first members of the recently-founded California Newspaper Hall of Fame.

47

Joel Pickens Walker

Joel was born on November 20, 1797, in Goochland County Virginia, the third of seven children. His grandfather was born in Ireland, brought to America as a young boy, and fought in the American Revolution. By 1798, the family was living in Roane Tennessee. Joel was one year old when brother Joseph, the future legendary frontiersman, was born. Their father died when Joel was 12 years old.

In February 1824, 26-year-old Joel married 24-year-old Mary Young and settled into farming life in Independence Missouri. On May 21, 1827, he was sworn in as the first justice of the peace.

In May 1832, Joel joined his brother and 110 other experienced hunters and trappers on the four-year-long exploring expedition led by Benjamin Bonneville. Joseph led a party of men to explore the Great Salt Lake and find an overland route to California. He discovered a route along the Humboldt River across present-day Nevada, as well as Walker Pass across the Sierra Nevada. He established an essential segment of the California Trail.

Joel returned to Missouri; but in 1840, he set out for Oregon with his wife and four children, joining a party of fur traders and missionaries. They arrived in Willamette Valley in September 1840, but departed the following September for California and New Helvetia, traveling this time with the Navy.

In 1841, a U.S. Navy charting expedition was ordered to travel overland on the Siskiyou Trail from Oregon to Sutter's New Helvetia. With them was a group of settlers, including the Joel Walker family.

They arrived at Sutter's Fort in October 1841, while the Fort was still under construction. Joel found work at Sutter's Mill as a manager and drover. When John Sutter accepted the Russians' offer to purchase all the cattle and goods at the shuttered Fort Ross, Joel acted as his agent during the removal.

Two years later, the Walkers returned to Oregon, this time bringing cattle and horses which they sold to incoming settlers. But, in 1848, they returned to California, buying farmland near Sebastopol in Sonoma County where Joel opened a store—and never moved again.

At the Constitutional Convention, Joel was appointed to the finance committee. Outside of having his name appear on the roll call votes, on September 25, William Gwin cited Joel's report on land grants for school sites in Oregon.

After the Convention, Joel accepted a nomination for senator representing Sonoma but was not elected.

In August 1856, his wife, Mary, died at age 56. In September 1864, the 66-year-old widower married 59-year-old Eveline Middleton.

In their later years, the Walker brothers seemed to enjoy a certain celebrity status as living frontier legends. Newspapers frequently printed the reminiscences and anecdotes Joel and Joseph would share when they happen to drop by the newspaper offices for a chat. Joseph died in October 1876 at the age of 77. Joel died on June 25, 1879, at the age of 82.

48

Mariano Guadalupe Vallejo

The eighth of 13 children, Mariano was born in Monterey on July 7, 1807. His family came to California under rather dramatic circumstances.

His grandparents had emigrated from northern Spain to Guadalajara Mexico where his father Ignacio was expected to join the holy community. But, on the day of his ordination, he created a scene—arguing with the officiating clergyman, throwing off his sacerdotal vestments and choosing his own destiny in the military.

The company Ignacio joined was escorting Father Junipero Serra into Alta California in 1769. As military commissioner and engineer, Ignacio was later sent north to Petaluma where he worked for years in planning and superintending the building of fortifications, laying out the various towns of the territory, and directing the construction of the irrigating canals and waterworks of the missions.

Mariano's legacy was no less extraordinary than his father's, beginning with his training. He received an excellent education, first from William Hartnell, a friend of his father's who taught him English, French and Latin; then from the Spanish Governor of Alta California, Pablo Vicente de Sola. Mariano was serving as personal secretary to the new Governor Luis Argüello when news of Mexico's independence from Spain reached Monterey. Argüello enrolled Mariano as a military cadet in the Presidio Company in 1824.

In March 1832, 24-year-old Mariano married 15-year-old Francisca Benicia Carrillo in San Diego. The couple became parents to 16 children.

In 1833, Governor Figueroa received instructions from the Mexican National Government to establish a strong presence in the region north of the San Francisco Bay to protect the area from the encroachment of foreigners. Figueroa named Lieutenant Vallejo as military commander of the Northern Frontier, to order the soldiers, arms and material at the Presidio of San Francisco moved to the site of the recently secularized Mission San Francisco Solano.

The governor granted Mariano approximately 40,000 acres of Rancho Petaluma, immediately west of Sonoma. He also named him director of colonization which meant that he could initiate land grants for other colonists subject to approval by the governor and the legislature.

Mariano was instructed by the governor to establish a pueblo at the site of the old mission. In 1835, the streets, lots, central plaza and a broad main avenue for the new Pueblo de Sonoma were laid out. Yet, Sonoma remained under military control. In 1843, Vallejo, now lieutenant colonel, wrote to the governor recommending that a civil government be organized for Sonoma. The next year a Town Council was established.

When Governor Micheltoreno was exiled from California in

1845, he ordered Mariano to join him with the forces under his command. Mariano refused, saying he did not wish to fight his friends and relations. Alvarado and Castro, the chief leaders of the revolutionists, were his nephews.

Despite his high rank, Mariano was extremely critical of much of the Mexican upper-class society and government. He consistently identified with Mexican liberals, who stressed the rule of law and an efficient government with constitutionally limited powers, separate from religious authority.

In March 1846, one month before Congress declared war on Mexico, Governor Pio Pico called a convention of leading citizens at Santa Barbara to decide the future of Alta California. The stronger majority party were in favor of an English protectorate while Mariano's minority party was in favor of an independent republic, ultimately joining the American Union. He believed the best hope for California's economic and cultural development was with the United States.

Unable to reach a decision, the convention leaders scheduled another meeting. Mariano was aware that the members of the majority party would lobby the minority members to bring a vote in favor of British protection. To prevent this from happening, he intentionally created hostile feelings between the other leading citizens which resulted in the convention being disbanded indefinitely.

As military commander of the Northern Frontier, Mariano had been meeting secretly with Thomas Larkin, the confidential representative of the United States, to negotiate the United States' peaceful annexation of Alta California.

With the details worked out, Thomas's dispatch to Congress was en route when war with Mexico was declared.

During the Constitutional Convention, Mariano frequently suggested regulations that were law under the previous Mexican government. He wanted to prevent the body politic from Americanizing California.

September 28. On motion of Mr. Gwin, the resolution offered some days ago by Mr. Vallejo was taken up, viz,

Resolved, that three Commissioners be elected by ballot to draft a code of laws for the government of California, to be submitted to the Legislature for their approval at the first session thereof. (The following day the matter was reintroduced, debated and voted down. It was the delegates' opinion that the task was too immense, even though a code of laws was essential to the process.)

After the Constitutional Convention, Mariano was elected a state senator and succeeded in persuading the legislature to move the state capital to Vallejo. The legislature did meet there in 1852. Dissatisfied with the accommodations, they voted to move the capital to Benicia, another city that Mariano had assisted in developing on his expansive rancho property.

When Reverend Walter Colton's book, *Three Years in California* was published in July 1850, the dedication further assured Mariano's place in California history. "To General Mariano Guadalupe Vallejo, one of California's distinguished sons, in whom the interests of freedom, humanity, and education have found an able advocate and munificent benefactor, this volume is most respectfully dedicated by his friend the author."

Mariano adapted easily to the American occupation. The Yankee way of doing things appealed to his secular, progressive instincts. He sent his son Platon to New York to attend Columbia's College of Physicians and Surgeons. Graduating at the head of this class, Platon Vallejo was the first Spanish-speaking Californian to earn a Doctor of Medicine degree. He later served in the medical corps of the Union Army during the Civil War.

From the 1860s onward, Mariano held a place of affectionate importance in the imagination of American California. He symbolized the hope that all of the old California had not been lost. His presence brought an aura of old California to official gatherings.

A lengthy legal challenge to Mariano's land title cost him thousands of dollars in legal fees and finally deprived him of almost all his land. But, in September 1862, the United States District Court confirmed his grant of the 3,200-acre Rancho Agua Caliente in Solano County.

In 1865, Mariano visited the East Coast, where he was received in Washington with great admiration and respect by his old California acquaintances. Wanting to show that he considered everyone he met his equal, he called them all by their first names. He assured Abraham [Lincoln] of the loyalty of the California Spanish-speaking population.

Mariano's last home was the 56-acre Lachryma Montis in Sonoma. The two-story, wood frame house was designed and built on the East Coast in 1851, shipped around the Cape Horn and re-assembled at the present site. The style is Gothic Victorian, ... each room having its own white marble fireplace. The crystal chandeliers, lace curtains, rosewood grand piano, and many other furnishings were imported from Europe. Grape vines and fruit trees were planted around the estate. For several years, his wines and brandies took the First Premium at the State Fairs, and at the

Mechanic's Fairs in San Francisco. The quarter-mile-long driveway entrance was lined with cottonwood trees and Castilian roses.

Unlike Manuel Dominguez, Mariano willingly contributed to Hubert Howe Bancroft's *History of California*.

<u>February 1875</u>. General Vallejo at Home. The gentleman ... spent two days in the office of General Vallejo whom he found busy at work upon the history of this country. The history of the General's writing begins with the arrival in San Diego of Capt. Rivera Moncada [in 1769] and will reach up to 1848. Our informant, who has been allowed the privilege of perusing the interesting manuscript, informs us that there already written 1,000 pages of 300 words to each page, and history is complete up to 1836. ... It is the current report that the precious manuscript will, when completed, be donated to the Bancroft Library.

<u>March 1882</u>. Golden wedding. ... Gen. Mariano Vallejo and his estimable wife are one of the few but fortunate couples who a long half-century of wedded life ... Finds them closer. Monday of last week marked the General's 50th anniversary which he intended celebrating quietly with his family at his delightful home in Sonoma Valley. But although kept exceedingly quiet, at the last moment, it got out. The American flag was at once raised in the Plaza and by all citizens having flagstaffs. In the evening a large number of his friends and fellow citizens with a band of music and armed with a gold-headed cane laid siege to the General's castle which soon capitulated and admitted them. After music, seated about the dining room table, toasts sandwiched with cake and wine and short speeches that occasionally recalled amusing bits of early history were received with a keen relish. Dr. Ball, who had been delegated to deliver the cane presented it with an appropriate address which the General, filled with emotion at the complementary and appreciative utterances of his friends, delivered a hearty and feeling response. ...

On January 18, 1890, Mariano died peacefully after a lingering illness. He was 82 years old. His wife of 58 years, Francisca Benicia, would die the following year.

Reference Sources

A Pictorial and Narrative History of Monterey; Jeanne Van Nostrand
A Scotch Paisano: Hugo Reid's Life in California; Susanna Dakin
A Trip to the Gold Mines of California in 1848; John A. Swan
Americans and the California Dream; Kevin Starr
Ancestry.com
Archive.org
Arlingtoncemetery.net/
Biography of First California Legislature; Sacramento Society of California Pioneers
bioguide.congress.gov
Boys' Book of Frontier Fighters, a Fracas on the Santa Fe Trail; E. Sabin
California; Kevin Starr
California; Joshua Royce
California Blue Book, State Roster 1909; Charles Forrest Curry
California CAGenWeb Archives
Calif. Digital Newspaper Collection; UCR-Center for Bibliographical Studies & Research
California Historical Society Quarterly
Chile, Peru, and the California Gold Rush of 1849; Jay Monaghan
Civil War Trust
Congressional Record: Proceedings and Debates, Vol. 21, Part 4
Covered Wagon Women, Diaries and Letters; edited by K. L. Holmes
Daily Alta California newspaper

El Dorado – Adventures in the Path of Empire; Bayard Taylor

FamousAmericans.net

For the People — Inside the Los Angeles County District Attorney's Office 1850-2000; Michael Parrish

Founding the Far West – California, Oregon and Nevada; D. Johnson

From Cowhides to Golden Fleece; Reuben Lukens Underhill

Frontiersman to Statesman; Benjamin S Lippincott

"General Bennet Riley, Commandant at Fort Gibson and Gov. of California;" Carolyn Thomas Foreman (Chronicles of Oklahoma)

Gold Rush Port; James Delgado

Governors.library.ca.gov

"Guard Duty And Court-Martials: Gen. Bennet Riley;" R. Friesen

"Henry Wager Halleck; " Judge T. W. Freelon

Historical Articles of Solano County: Online Database

History of San Joaquin County, with Biographical Sketches; G. Tinkham

History of the State of California and Biographical Record; James Guinn

History of Warren County; edited By H. P. Smith

Islapedia.com

JoinCalifornia.com

Journal and Reports of Major Bennet Riley and Lieutenant Philip St. George Cooke; Otis E. Young

"Journal of the Proceedings of the House of Assembly of the State of California at Its First Session"

Knox County Historical Society

Lafayette Historical Society

Land & Water Laws of Mexico & California; Mariano Galván Rivera

Library of Congress

Life of Stephen Foster; H. .D Barrows

Mariposaresearch.net

McCarver and Tacoma; Virginia M. & Thomas Prosch

Media Museum of Northern California

Memoires of Elisha Oscar Crosby; Charles Albro Barker, Editor

Memorial and Biographical History of the Coast Counties of Central California; Henry Barrows & Luther Ingersoll, Editors
Men to Match My Mountains; Irving Stone
Monterey County: the dramatic story of its past; Augustus Fink
Narciso Botello's Annals of Southern California; Brent C. Dickerson
National Governors Association
Negotiating Conquest; Miroslava Chavez-Garcia
Oldcitycemetery.com/cholera.htm
Oliver M. Wozencraft in California, 1849-1887; Barbara Ann Metcalf
"Ord Street: the Soldier, the Surveyor ...;" Elisabeth L. Uyeda
"Pacific Historical Review;" H. Brett Melendy
Pasadena Star News
Physical Proofs of Another Life; Francis James Lippitt
Recollections of California, 1846-1861; General William T. Sherman
Recollections of General Halleck, as Secretary of State in Monterey, 1847-9; Rev. H. S. Willey
Recollections of Historical Events, 1843-1878; William A. Streeter
"Remembering Anaheim's History;" J'aime Rubio
Reminiscences of Francis J. Lippitt; Francis J. Lippitt
Report of the debates in the Convention of California, on the Formation of the State Constitution; J. Ross Browne
Representative & Leading Men of the Pacific; Oscar T. Shuck
"Ripples of Hope: Great American Civil Rights Speeches;" Josh Gottheimer
"Robert Baylor Semple, Pioneer;" Zoe Green Radcliffe
Sacramento Daily Union newspaper
San Diego History.org
San Francisco Call newspaper
San Francisco Chronicle newspaper
San Jose Pioneer newspaper
Santa Barbara Historical Museum
Santa Barbara Independent newspaper
Sfgenealogy.com

Sixty Years in Southern California, 1853-1913; Harris Newmark
Smithsonian Institute Libraries
Sonoma Wine and the Story of Buena Vista; Charles L. Sullivan
Socialarchive.iath.virginia.edu
Supreme.Justia.com
Testimonios; Rose Marie Beebe & Robert Senkewicz
The American Whig Review
The Bay of San Francisco
The Congressional Globe, Volume 50, Part 2, November 1917
The Early Days and Men of California; William F Swasey
The Emigrants Guide to Oregon and California; Lansford W. Hastings
The Genesis of California's First Constitutional Convention; R. D. Hunt
The Governors of New Jersey: Biographical Essays; Micheal Birkner
The Journal of Lt. J. M. Hollingsworth; J. M. H. Hollingsworth
The Mountain Democrat newspaper
The Presidio of San Francisco, A History; Erwin M. Thompson
The Struggle for Civil Government in California, 1846-1850; J. Ellison
The Transition Period of California; Rev. Samuel H. Willey
Thirty Years in California, 1849 to 1879; Rev. S. H. Willey
Three Years in California; Walter Colton
To the Golden Shore: America Goes to California, 1849; P. Browning
"Two Letters of James McHall Jones;" James McCall Jones
Unholy Traffic in Human Blood and Souls; Benjamin Medley
Virginia Biographical Encyclopedia
Wherever There's a Fight; Elaine Elinson and Stan Yogi